PREACHING: A KIND OF FOLLY

PREACHING:
A KIND OF FOLLY

BY

IAN PITT-WATSON

THE WESTMINSTER PRESS

PHILADELPHIA

First published by The Saint Andrew Press,
Edinburgh, Scotland under the title
A Kind of Folly : Toward a Practical Theology of Preaching

Published by The Westminster Press ®
Philadelphia, Pennsylvania

PRINTED IN THE UNITED STATES OF AMERICA
9 8 7 6 5 4 3 2 1

Library of Congress Cataloging in Publication Data

Pitt-Watson, Ian, 1921–
   Preaching.

   First published in 1976 under title: A kind of folly.
   Based on the Warrack lectures delivered by the author
between 1972 and 1975 at the universities of St. Andrews,
Edinburgh, Aberdeen, and Glasgow.
   1. Preaching. I. Title.
   BV4211.2.P55 1978   251   77-21983
   ISBN 0-664-24181-6

CONTENTS

PREFACE

Frank Warrack (who established 'The Preacher's Lectureship' in 1924) would have been shocked to see the address at the end of this preface and the occupation of the author. With refreshing bluntness he required that Professors of the Colleges of the Church should be expressly excluded from holding his Lectureship. The terms of the Trust have not, however, been violated. The invitation to give the Warrack Lectures came to me when I was still fully committed to the preaching and pastoral ministry. By that time I had spent fifteen ·exciting, rewarding and exhausting years in the service of two large congregations—first at St James's, Forfar, and latterly at New Kilpatrick, Bearsden. It was against the background of that experience and the pressures of that commitment that the lectures were prepared which form the substance of this book.

If I were to rewrite the material now I might express myself rather differently. I would certainly not expose myself to the embarrassment of the final section. But I suspect that the rewritten material, though it might appear a little more responsible academically, would lose whatever practical value it may have in terms of Frank Warrack's intention. So I have allowed the original draft to stand with the minimum of editing. In consequence this book is no more than the clumsy attempt of a hard-pressed parish minister to assess theologically his own preaching practice. It is what Barth calls 'the description of this embarrassment'.

Our concern here is with preaching in its traditional form. Had time allowed I would have wished to develop the theological argument further in terms of other forms of communication, both verbal and non-verbal. In this regard the section on 'Preaching and the Will' and 'Preaching and the Emotions' would have been especially relevant. I would also have wished to develop the central theological argument in terms of the inter-dependence of preaching, worship and pastoral care; for I am convinced that the failure to recognise that interdependence inevitably leads to a distortion of all three. So our single-minded concern here with preaching in its traditional form is in response to the clearly stated intention of the Warrack Trust and does not imply disinterest in these wider and still more important issues.

I am grateful to the Trustees of the Warrack Lectureship for inviting me to undertake this task and I much appreciated the warmth of the response I received when the Lectures were given in St Mary's College, St Andrews, New College, Edinburgh, Trinity College, Glasgow and Christ's College, Aberdeen. My thanks are also due to my good friend and colleague Rev. Dr. James S. Wood who revised the proofs.

My debt to my distinguished predecessors in this Lectureship is a very real and personal one for I have been privileged to number many of them among my friends and all of them in some measure have been my teachers. My debt to the members of St James's Church, Forfar and New Kilpatrick Church, Bearsden is an even greater one for they taught me a kind of Christian understanding and Christian witness that goes beyond ideas conceived in the study and words spoken from the pulpit. But my greatest indebtedness is to my own father, who, in my boyhood days, seemed to me to be indisputably the greatest preacher in the world, and who still, for weal or woe, remains the greatest influence on my life. To his memory this book is dedicated with affection and gratitude.

Christs College   IAN PITT-WATSON
Aberdeen

1

INTRODUCTION
A KIND OF FOLLY

1. Practical Doubts

In an inspired mistranslation the Authorised Version of the Bible speaks of 'the foolishness of preaching' (1 Cor. 1:21). For Paul the foolishness is a characteristic of the Gospel itself, not just of our presentation of it. It is God's foolishness not ours that is 'wiser than men'. Yet I believe the mistranslation says something true, for surely part of 'the folly of the Gospel' is 'the foolishness of preaching' (See 1 Cor. 2:4). Certainly our weekly pulpit monologues are a kind of folly and it is not surprising that many ministers and theological students have begun to ask radical questions about their purpose and effectiveness. Preaching is supposed to be proclaiming the mighty acts of God. Is this only or even primarily to be done by one man talking from a pulpit Sunday after Sunday to the same little group of people? Is it not rather the responsibility of the whole people of God, in dialogue one with another and with the world, to seek God's will, and, having found it to embody the Gospel in action to meet the world's needs? Will the world listen to any other language? 'Don't preach' is recognised by all the secular communicators as a condition of successful persuasion—or, at least, 'don't be seen to preach'. Isn't it about time the Church got the message? The day of the preacher is past, the day of the discussion group has come and almost gone, the day of the action group and of the non-verbal communicator is here.

Reinforcing arguments are not hard to find. Talk politics and one finds that dogma, propaganda and the party line are all tarred with the same brush and oratory is a dirty word. Talk educational psychology and one finds that the preacher's total dependence on the unchallenged spoken word breaks every rule in the book. Talk ethics and one may doubt whether any average man should be subjected to such a weekly public disclosure of the gulf between what he stands for and what he is. Talk liturgics and one may well believe that our sermon-centred tradition of worship in the Church of Scotland (to which I belong) has gravely impoverished the devotional life of its members.

Add to that a profound uncertainty about what we should be saying and our authority in saying it. There is no real theological consensus within the Church of Scotland and any attempt to impose more explicit doctrinal standards on the Church is strenuously and, I think, rightly resisted. The divinity colleges themselves have each their own special ethos. What is taught in one is challenged in another. And within each college a wide divergence of belief is to be found. I am not lamenting this, indeed I welcome it. But the fact remains that the average preacher is left with an uncomfortable feeling that though he may boldly begin his sermon 'In the name of the Father and of the Son and of the Holy Spirit' the truth of the matter is that he has been left to play his own intellectual and spiritual hunches. Sometimes he may doubt the validity of these even for himself.

In other words, the preacher finds himself landed with an authoritarian task, lacking the authority to carry it to a successful conclusion. Once the preacher

2

could rest upon the verbal authority of the Bible he preached and the doctrinal authority of the church which had ordained him. Neither authority is any longer accepted by his hearers nor would the preacher wish to have it otherwise. Once the preacher had a recognised authority given him in matters of morals and manners as the natural consequence of his secure and clearly defined place in the established structure of society; that period too is gone and we can only hope it is not sour grapes when we say we believe ourselves to be well rid of it. Less happily, however, we have lost another kind of authority—the intellectual authority which preachers of the past often enjoyed. The nineteenth century pulpit lifted a man six feet above contradiction not simply because he was a minister but because he was a much better educated and better informed man than the majority of people to whom he was speaking. That is no longer the case for many of us. One can of course adduce theological reasons to suggest that this intellectual advantage which preachers once enjoyed was a counterfeit authority which we are well quit of with the rest—'God chose the foolish things of the world to confound the wise'. But I suspect this would be no more than a rationalisation, and certainly no one would use this as an excuse to justify an uneducated ministry.

So, lacking alike the authority of the Biblical literalist, the ecclesiastical dogmatist and the intellectual aristocrat, on what authority does the preacher now find himself driven back? The answer should, of course, be 'on the authority of the Word of God vivified by the work of the Holy Spirit'. But the Word of God for the preacher is none other than his own convictions of what the Word of God is to him, and the work of the Holy Spirit for him means primarily his own experience of God. A man cannot honestly preach what he does not himself believe nor can he adequately speak of what he has not himself experienced. So the preacher finds himself limited by the flimsiness of his own convictions and the narrow range of his own religious experience. No wonder he often feels tongue-tied and inhibited. Then, if he is wise, he will remember his ordination and the nature of his calling: that 'he is not (to paraphrase Kant) a gentleman volunteer in the army of the Lord but a conscript subject to the full rigours of camp life'.

But still there are very many men in the preaching ministry of the Church who know only too well that ordination does not provide some kind of professional immunity to doubt but who are fighting a daily battle for their spiritual and intellectual lives. Without such men in its ministry the Church would be seriously impoverished. I am not thinking just now about the convinced theological radical. He has his own vital contribution to make to the intellectual life of the Church and also his own special problems of conscience as a preacher. But he is in a relatively small minority. I am thinking primarily of the larger minority within the ordained ministry (among whom I number myself) who pray or ought to pray 'Lord I believe, help thou my unbelief'. Such men too must preach. Little wonder that sometimes we ask 'Must we?' Are there not other and better ways in which God can use us in the service of his kingdom?

I hope I have said enough to show that I am not without sympathy for those who would gladly be quit of the burden of preaching or who at least would like to see that burden lightened. I don't understand preaching. I am not even clear in my own mind what I am trying to do in preaching—and that, I know, is a dangerous admission. But I am convinced that a constraint is laid upon me not just by the tradition of the church to which I happen to belong but by the nature of the Christ-event itself. Part of the folly of the Gospel is the foolishness of preaching and 'it pleased God by the foolishness of preaching to save them that believe'—to continue with the inspired mistranslation of the Authorised Version! I don't understand preaching, but I believe in it deeply and I am convinced that our present scepticism—cynicism even—concerning the value of preaching is a dangerous threat to the life and witness of the Church. We've lost our nerve and it is time we got it back.

2. Theological Reassurances

The reasons for this lack of nerve are not theological. Characteristic of the theology of the twentieth century has been a clear and explicit recognition of the importance of preaching. When Kahler declared in 1886 'the real Christ is the preached Christ' he was not simply calling a halt to the misplaced optimism of the nineteenth century liberal quest for the historical Jesus; he was pointing theology in a new direction which Barth and Bultmann were to follow together—to the immense profit of the Church, however much they might dispute with one another about where the road was leading them. The real Christ was no longer to be thought of as a shadowy Jesus of Nazareth precariously resurrected and revivified by the professional historians. The real Christ was to be found in the proclamation of the Church. Thus preaching came to be seen as more than a popular restatement for the theologically innocent of what the theologians were already saying more subtly and more precisely to one another. Preaching was seen to be not merely the end product of theological endeavour but at the same time the raw material with which it was working. The main thrust of twentieth century theological thought has taught us—or so it seems to me—that preaching is, quite literally, the beginning and the end of theology.

It certainly was so for Karl Barth. As early as 1922 speaking to a meeting of ministers he said this:

'... For twelve years I was a minister, as all of you are. I *had* my theology. It was not really mine, to be sure, but that of my unforgotten teacher Wilhelm Hermann, grafted upon the principles which I had learned, less consciously than unconsciously, in my native home—the principles of those Reformed Churches which today I represent and am honoured to represent in an official capacity. Once in the ministry, I found myself growing away from these theological habits of thought and being forced back at every point more and more upon the specific *minister's* problem, the *sermon*. I sought to find my way between the problem of human life on the one hand and the content of the Bible on the other. As a minister I wanted to speak to the *people* in the infinite contradiction of their life, but to speak the no less infinite message of the *Bible*, which was as much of a riddle as life. Often enough these two magnitudes, life and the Bible, have risen before me (and still rise!) like Scylla and Charybdis: if *these* are the whence and whither of Christian preaching, who shall, who can, be a minister and preach? I am sure that you all know this situation and this difficulty ...

6

It simply came about that the familiar situation of the minister on Saturday at his desk and on Sunday in his pulpit crystallized in my case into a marginal note to all theology, which finally assumed the voluminous form of a complete commentary upon the Epistle to the Romans; and events have taken a similar course with my friends.

It is not as if I had found any way out of this critical situation. *Exactly not that.* But this critical situation itself became to me an explanation of the character of all theology. What else can theology be but the truest possible expression of this quest and questioning on the part of the minister, the description of this embarrassment. . . .' (*The Word of God and the Word of Man,* pp. 100–101)

That passage vividly reflects the experience of many in the ministry of the Church including some (like myself) who do not always find the climate of Barth's thought so congenial.

From radically different premises for radically different reasons, Rudolph Bultmann arrives at the same conclusion regarding the centrality of preaching. For him, also, preaching is the beginning and the end of theology: the beginning, since revelation is to be found in the preaching of the Church *and nowhere else;* the end, since all theology true to the New Testament must have the characteristic of existential address. Accordingly, John Macquarrie writes:

'Bultmann therefore adheres to the importance of preaching in the Protestant and Evangelical tradition. In the proclamation of the Word, it is the risen Christ, yes, God himself who speaks. Grace is present in the proclamation, the saving deed itself is present, for as saving deed it is an eschatological or existential-historical event and therefore not tied to a particular point in time. This high concept of preaching is, of course, found in the New Testament. "We are ambassadors for Christ, as though God did beseech you by us: we pray you in Christ's stead be ye reconciled to God." The Word which is proclaimed is God's Word, and in it God speaks to men, as he spoke in the Incarnate Word.

Here also there is a definite view of what preaching ought to do. Its function is to bring men into the moment of decision, to disclose to them their own selves in the light of the cross and resurrection. From what we know of apostolic preaching in the New Testament, Bultmann again would appear to be loyal here to the New Testament understanding of preaching. It is an *existentiell* proclamation which brings the hearer to confront the gift of grace. True, much has passed for preaching in the Church that would not conform to this understanding of it, but that is a judgement of what the Church has made of the gift of the Word entrusted to it. It would not be too much to say that the whole aim of Bultmann's theology, including his views on demythologizing, is to spotlight the essential *kerygma* of the New Testament for the men and women of our time, and to bring it before them as the one relevant possibility that is still open for a bewildered world. His aim, that is to say, is an evangelical one.' (*An Existentialist Theology*, pp. 225–226)

For Paul Tillich, the Church's preaching is not the starting point as it was in different ways for both Barth and Bultmann. But, in the end, Tillich is perhaps the most persuasive advocate of the three for the thesis that preaching is or ought to be central to the Church's life. He *talks* less than some others of his contemporaries

8

about the theological significance of preaching, but he *does* it better than any of them. Any man who has come to doubt whether the sermon can still be an effective instrument of communication in the modern world would do well to read or re-read the sermons of Paul Tillich. An ounce of example is worth a ton of precept, so let us take a specific passage and examine it in some detail. In this familiar passage Tillich is preaching about grace:

'. . . There is too often a graceless acceptance of Christian doctrines and a graceless battle against the structures of evil in our personalities. Such a graceless relation to God may lead us by necessity either to arrogance or to despair. It would be better to refuse God and the Christ and the Bible than to accept Them without grace. For if we accept without grace, we do so in the state of separation, and can only succeed in deepening the separation. We cannot transform our lives, unless we allow them to be transformed by that stroke of grace. It happens; or it does not happen. And certainly it does *not* happen if we try to force it upon ourselves, just as it shall not happen so long as we think, in our self-complacency, that we have no need of it. Grace strikes us when we are in great pain and restlessness. It strikes us when we walk through the dark valley of a meaningless and empty life. It strikes us when we feel that our separation is deeper than usual, because we have violated another life, a life which we loved, or from which we were estranged. It strikes us when our disgust for our own being, our indifference, our weakness, our hostility, and our lack of direction and composure have become intolerable to us. It strikes us when, year after year, the longed-for perfection of life does not appear, when the old compulsions reign within us as they have for decades, when despair destroys all joy and courage. Sometimes at that moment a wave of light breaks into our darkness, and it is as though a voice were saying: "You are accepted. *You are accepted,* accepted by that which is greater than you, and the name of which you do not know. Do not ask for the name now; perhaps you will find it later. Do not try to do anything now; perhaps later you will do much. Do not seek for anything; do not perform anything; do not intend anything. *Simply accept the fact that you are accepted!*" If that happens to us, we experience grace. After such an experience we may not be better than before, and we may not believe more than before. But everything is transformed. In that moment, grace conquers sin, and reconciliation bridges the gulf of estrangement. And nothing is demanded of this experience, no religious or moral or intellectual presupposition, nothing but *acceptance.*' (*The Shaking of the Foundations* pp. 161–162)

I believe that that is great preaching and merits careful and detailed analysis. Admittedly it is 'academic' preaching in the sense that it is addressed primarily to an undergraduate audience; yet the language is simple and the sentence-structure terse. It is profoundly Biblical and theological preaching, an exposition of one word, 'Grace'; yet it is not content to rest on Biblical and theological images or vocabulary but reaches out boldly to express its meaning in the currency of contemporary speech and experience. One is reminded of Barth's Scylla and Charybdis for the preacher, 'the problem of human life on the one hand, the content of the Bible on the other'. Tillich here has found the way between the two. Barth said, 'As a minister I wanted to speak to people in the infinite contradiction of their life, but to speak the no less infinite message of the *Bible* which was as much of a riddle as life'. Here Tillich does just that. Again Bultmann's view that preaching ought to disclose to men their own selves in the light of the *kerygma* is here vividly exemplified, and the evangelical motive behind his demythologising becomes apparent. . . . One final dangerous lesson is to be learned from the Tillich passage. It clearly and deliberately engages the emotions as well as the intellect. The italicised rhetorical repetitions make that abundantly clear; nor can one doubt that this emotional impact is part of the sermon's power.

So much one can see. But, in the end of the day, I suspect that the thing that makes it great preaching will defy analysis. Like grace, by grace, 'it happens or it does not happen'.

3. Identification of Objectives

However elusive the essence of great preaching may be it is worth trying to isolate and analyse the essential elements in it that *can* be identified. This we must now attempt to do with reference to the Tillich passage pp 9+10 already quoted. Certain guide-lines emerge.

First, this is biblical and theological preaching. If this element is missing, whatever else we are doing we are not engaged in Christian *preaching*. Our primary task is to speak not of what *we* think and feel and ought to do but of what *God* is and does. There is a simple but necessary discipline to which all our preaching should be subject. The question must always be asked 'What *doctrine* does this sermon seek to present and illuminate?' If no clear answer can be given to that

11

question the subject matter of the sermon must be suspect. All preaching should be doctrinal preaching. Of course this does not mean that it should be 'academic' or 'theological' in the narrow technical sense of that word. The bigger the truth we try to speak the smaller the words we should use, and the shorter the sentences. Nor does doctrinal preaching mean that we ignore the immediate practical and secular concerns of our hearers. On the contrary, we cannot preach an incarnational theology without involvement in these concerns. Nor does it mean that psychology and simple introspection have no place in the preacher's universe of discourse. What we feel is often more important than what we think. I am not unaware of the theological dangers of psychological preaching. But I am persuaded that often it is here—especially in the psychology of personal relationships (how people feel about one another)—that many of our hearers first discover what it is to think and feel 'in depth'. Part of our task is to point to what our hearers already know in their own experience, to identify *that* theologically and then to use the theological bridge-head thus established as a *base* from which we can break through into new theological truths which our hearers do *not* already know. By the same token it is a serious error to suppose that doctrinal preaching means that ethical problems are to be ignored. On the contrary. 'He that *doeth* the will of God shall know of the doctrine . . .' (John 7:17). The questions our hearers are asking are ethical rather than theological questions. We must be prepared to meet them at their own point of concern. Nor should we be afraid of moral exhortation and even moral condemnation—so long as we make it clear that it is ourselves as well as our hearers whom we seek to exhort or condemn. Reaction in our own day against this kind

12

of preaching has been sharp and necessary but has gone far enough. Moral concern expressed in terms of contrition is sometimes a necessary prolegomena to true hearing of the gospel and moral concern expressed as resolve is often the only appropriate response to it. But if between the contrition and the resolution there is no gospel, no *kerygma* then there is no preaching. It is in this sense that I would insist that *all* preaching should be doctrinal. The time spent speaking specifically about the doctrine may be a relatively small part of the whole sermon; indeed in some cases the doctrine may never be explicitly identified in traditional terms at all. But the doctrine must be there or we are not doing our job.

This leads on to a further point again admirably exemplified by the Tillich passage. To say that all preaching should be Biblical and theological does not mean that, once we have homed in on the traditional doctrinal truth we are trying to illuminate, and have expressed it in Biblical or theological language, our task is done. On the contrary it is precisely here that our real task often begins. Once again I'm aware of the theological problems this raises. Is there perhaps after all, as Barth maintains, a 'language of Canaan', a special biblical-theological, God-given language in which alone we can speak with any assurance about God? If so the psychological hermeneutic of Schleiermacher and Dilthey is valueless. The preacher-interpreter who tries to project himself and his hearers into the experience of the Biblical writer he is expounding is simply wasting his time. But, more important, if the psychological hermeneutic of Schleiermacher and Dilthey is valueless the theological hermeneutic of Bultmann is positively dangerous, for Bultmann has made his existentialist hermeneutic the whole of theology. I am persuaded there is a middle way between Barth's biblical positivism in which *nothing* is to be translated from 'the language of Canaan' and Bultmann's full-blooded existentialism in which everything is to be translated. I am prepared to admit that no translation can be made without some distortion of meaning and that if we wholly lose touch with the original vocabulary and imagery of the Bible we will soon find ourselves groping. But I must still insist that an essential element in preaching is precisely this task of translating Biblical words and images into the coinage of contemporary language and contemporary experience. More, I believe that even if we preachers sometimes do this badly it is better that we should do it badly than not do it at all. If we take our evangelical responsibility seriously it is the Church's job to speak to the world in the world's language. It is no good telling the world that before it can hear it must first learn the language of the Church. It is our job to do the translation. Our translation will be imperfect and in some ways positively misleading. But once we have captured the interest of our hearers and engaged their concern we can point them back to the original so that they for themselves can learn the special Biblical theological language which Barth calls 'the language of Canaan'.

When I was a student of philosophy I was required in my first year to start reading the works of Immanuel Kant. One book by A. D. Lindsay we were strictly forbidden to read. We were told it was unreliable and misleading. It did however have the advantage of being intelligible which none of the other books prescribed were. I read it avidly but in secret. It gave me *some* understanding of what Kant was talking about as a whole. Only having read and understood my unreliable

14

but intelligible primer was I able to go on to better books and to the understanding of the original text itself. I would be happy if I could feel that my own preaching could fulfil that same limited function. But I see in the preaching of others a vividness and precision of translation which needs no such apology. Take Tillich's sermon again: 'Simply accept the fact that you are accepted. If that happens to us we experience grace'. That is the kind of hermeneutic that every preacher should admire and seek to emulate.

The next lesson to be learned from the Tillich passage is the skill with which it finds a way between Barth's Scylla and Charybdis, 'the problem of human life on the one hand, the content of the Bible on the other'. The problem of human life is there.

> 'Grace strikes us when we are in great pain and restlessness. It strikes us when we walk through the dark valley of a meaningless and empty life. It strikes us when we feel that our separation is deeper than usual, because we have violated another life, a life which we loved, or from which we were estranged. It strikes us when our disgust for our own being, our indifference, our weakness, our hostility, and our lack of direction and composure have become intolerable to us. It strikes us when, year after year, the longed-for perfection of life does not appear, when the old compulsions reign within us as they have for decades, when despair destroys all joy and courage' (loc. cit. pp. 161-2).

But in immediate and relevant juxtaposition to these 'problems of human life' Tillich sets 'the content of the Bible'.

> 'Sometimes at that moment a wave of light breaks into our darkness, and it as though a voice were saying:

15

"You are accepted. *You are accepted,* accepted by that which is greater than you, and the name of which you do not know. Do not ask for the name now; perhaps you will find it later. Do not try to do anything now; perhaps later you will do much. Do not seek for anything; do not perform anything; do not intend anything. *Simply accept the fact that you are accepted!*" If that happens to us, we experience grace. In that moment grace conquers sin' (loc. cit. p. 162).

The hermeneutic task has been so thoroughly undertaken that the language sounds quite unbiblical until the final sentence. But the authentic voice of Paul is heard throughout and so 'the content of the Bible' is proclaimed alongside 'the problem of human life'. Significantly these two elements which Barth describes in terms of opposition as Scylla and Charybdis, Tillich treats as natural allies. 'The problem of human life' can only be understood in the light of 'the content of the Bible'. But 'the content of the Bible' can only be understand once it has been embodied and experienced in 'the problem of human life'. Tillich summarises and concludes the sermon 'You are accepted' in these words: ' "Sin" and "grace" are strange words; but they are not strange things. We find them whenever we look into ourselves with searching eyes and longing hearts. They determine our life. They abound within us and in all of life. May grace more abound within us!' (loc. cit. p. 163).

In treating 'the problem of human life' and 'the content of the Bible' as natural allies Tillich refuses to accept the kind of compartmentalisation that has characterised much traditional doctrinal preaching. First the preacher states the doctrine in Biblical language and relates it to its Biblical context. Then

16

(unless he is prepared simply to state his thesis in 'the language of Canaan' without any translation) he goes on to interpret the Biblical doctrine in a language and imagery more familiar and intelligible to his hearers than the Biblical words and images with which he has begun. Finally, having thus elucidated what the doctrine means he proceeds to show its relevance to his hearers by applying it to the practical concerns of every day contemporary life. I am not suggesting that this is not a perfectly valid structure for a good sermon. What I *am* suggesting is that the doctrine we preach and the application of that doctrine to human life are not necessarily set on either side of a chasm which the preacher, with the aid of the Holy Spirit, must somehow try to bridge. Unless we are prepared to accept the *kerygma* as no more than a series of divinely inspired propositions, we will find the doctrine within the context of human life and experience or not at all. The doctrine cannot adequately be stated until it is applied. This is not to deny that there is a discontinuity between the human and the divine. It is simply to re-assert the old distinction between the order of knowing and the order of being. In the order of being, the chasm is there between the human and the divine. In the order of knowing, an incarnational theology must insist that 'the problem of human life' and 'the content of the Bible' are allies, not opposites. And it is with the order of knowing that the preacher is primarily concerned. In consequence, the exposition of the biblical doctrine and the application of that doctrine to contemporary life and experience are simply two facets of the same thing. For the sake of homiletical clarity and tidiness they can and often should be separated. But the separation of exposition from application which most sermons employ should not be allowed to conceal the fact that

17

exposition cannot be made without application and that the application is part of the exposition. In one sense all theology is practical theology.

This leads on naturally to a further point which we have already noted regarding the Tillich passage—his vivid demonstration of Bultmann's existentialist thesis that preaching ought to be an encounter in which men discover their own selves disclosed in the light of the *kerygma*.Tillich says: 'We find [sin and grace] whenever we look into ourselves with searching eyes and longing hearts'. On the face of it that looks a dangerously subjective conclusion to a sermon on a great Biblical theme. But this is the kind of subjectivity which, as an existentialist, Tillich is prepared not only to tolerate but to welcome. It is the subjectivity proper to the relationship of person to person in distinction from the objectivity of the relationship of person to thing. On the human level it is as person to persons (and in that sense subjectively) that the preacher speaks to his congregation. On the divine level it is as person to persons (and in that sense also subjectively) that God speaks through the preacher to preacher and congregation alike.

This latter point I believe is crucial. The preacher is himself addressed by his own preaching. 'I have received of the Lord that which also I delivered unto you' is a text relevant not only to the Ministry of the Sacrament but to the Ministry of the Word as well. Until God has spoken to us we have nothing to say. When the Word is preached it is not only preached *through* the preacher but *to* the preacher as well. It is essential that this be understood by both preacher and congregation. Without that understanding the preacher will remain objective to his subject matter and, however skilfully or eloquently he may manipulate it, real preaching will be impossible. Until the preacher is involved himself in what he is saying he is unlikely to involve others; until in some sense he has proved on his own pulses the truth of what he is saying he is unlikely to persuade others. This is one reason why plagiarism is to be deplored. It is not merely dishonest, it is self-destructive. Preaching requires a total identification of the man who speaks with what he says. Reading other men's sermons simply turns bad preachers into bad actors. Nor is plagiarism the only way in which the identification of the man who speaks with what he says can be lost. If we talk about different things in the pulpit from the things that concern us during the week; if we use a different kind of vocabulary and imagery; if the very tone of our voice is demonstrably different from the voice of the 'real' man who lives in the 'real' world, no one will listen to us, and rightly so. At best we will be regarded as some kind of professional medium—someone who claims that God is speaking *through* him and who therefore appropriately adopts a content and style of speech which is not his own. But if the preacher is not so much a medium *through* whom God speaks, as a *man* to whom God speaks, he must in turn speak with his own voice of those things which he himself has heard.

Of course there is a danger here of the wrong kind of subjectivity as there is a danger when Tillich says 'We find [sin and grace] whenever we look into ourselves with searching eyes and longing hearts'. Sometimes when we look into ourselves we find nothing but the reflection of our own dull faces which are of little interest to anyone but us and even to us are often depressing. But preaching is not an essay in spiritual autobiography, concerned with what *I* have thought, felt, done, suffered, enjoyed and believed. Preaching is

19

not about me. But neither can we say without the danger of misunderstanding that preaching is 'about' God. Merely to talk 'about' God is again to objectify him, to make him the object of our interest and enquiry. Our talking about God can of course be important and helpful and will be *part* of what the preacher is doing in every sermon. But the sermon, however interesting and informative, will have failed in its purpose unless at some point and in some way the preacher's words about God have become God's Word to him and through him to his hearers. It is essential for the integrity and sanity of the preacher that his congregation should know him as a man who is himself listening for that Word and being judged by it. He does not speak as one who has understood the Word far less as one who has obeyed it. But he *does* speak as one who has heard it and who seeks to hear more. He is not a man who addresses his congregation on the subject of God. Preacher and congregation alike are God's subjects, addressed by him.

This helps to explain a strange and welcome thing which is a commonplace of every preacher's experience. Sometimes he is thanked for a sermon he never consciously preached. The words he spoke have been appropriated to another man's personal situation in a way which the preacher himself had never thought of. Sometimes the preacher is told, encouragingly, 'You preached it specially to me'. He didn't. If he preached it specially to anyone it was probably to himself. (This is the subjectivity in the preacher's personal relationship with God which is not only to be tolerated but welcomed.) Yet what was heard was more than what was said, and for that 'more' we must always make room. It is a characteristic of all significant speech uttered within a real personal relationship that what is

20

said is seldom adequate to what is meant but that what is heard is often more than what is said. Otherwise talk between lovers would be impossible—or talk between God and man. When God speaks through the preacher, what is said is never adequate to express what is meant. But what is heard is often more than what is said. Perhaps sometimes if we said less more would be heard. Certainly the Word we preach is more than the words we say.

I said earlier that I didn't understand preaching. That at least will have been established by now. But that opening gambit was meant to be more than an apology in advance for the inadequacy of what was to follow. It was an assertion of something intrinsic to the nature of preaching. Because the preacher is involved in what he is saying and cannot be objective to it he can never fully understand what is happening when God speaks to him and through him. But he can be sure that this thing *does* happen, not always but sometimes, sufficiently often to make the preaching of the Word essential, even central, within his total ministry. *Why* it happens remains a mystery.

I don't understand preaching, but I believe in it as I believe in the Church of which it is a function. More, I am convinced that before a man can learn to preach he must first learn to believe in preaching. What I have tried to indicate so far is that, in spite of the practical problems confronting the preacher today, a belief in preaching is well grounded theologically and is central to the main thrust of twentieth century theological thought—liberal as well as conservative. If we have lost our faith in preaching it is not because the great Christian thinkers of our day have undermined that faith. On the contrary, they have sought to confirm it.

21

2

ARGUMENT:
TOWARD A PRACTICAL
THEOLOGY OF PREACHING

1. Theology and Preaching

Our present scepticism about the value of preaching
stems, I believe, from causes which are practical rather
than theological. The theological arguments all point
towards the urgent need for a recovery of our faith in
preaching. But practical arguments point in the
opposite direction. We've already looked briefly at some
of the practical difficulties. The chief one is that many
of us are not very good preachers. We are painfully
aware of our sheer technical incompetence for the job
we are trying to do. I want now to examine some of the
reasons for that feeling of incompetence.

Many of us are conscious that we are inadequately
equipped intellectually. We have already noted in
passing in the last lecture how the preacher today can
no longer assume that he has the intellectual head-start
over his hearers which once he had. Some of those to
whom he preaches may be better educated than he is;
some will certainly be more intelligent and better
informed. This is true not only of the middle class
congregation with a substantial number of professional
people in its membership. It is also true of congregations where professional people are conspicuous
by their absence. My own first charge was in Forfar.
There were 1700 members on the roll but only one
university graduate. My previous job had been six years

service as a University Chaplain. I knew *that* environment well since immediately previous to my appointment as Chaplain I had been a student myself for eight years. But I was profoundly concerned about my ability to adjust to a new environment of which I knew little or nothing. Preaching in University Chapel had been exciting and stimulating if not to the university congregation at least to myself. As I was required to preach only once every three weeks it was possible to allow, if necessary, two or three days for the preparation of a single sermon. Now it was to be twice a Sunday and preparation would have to be done in a matter of hours rather than days if the pastoral needs of a large congregation were to be met. Worst of all I had a fear that the kind of sermon I had been preaching in the university, which tried to come to grips with big theological issues, would be useless in this new non-academic set up. In one sense I was right: the language and imagery appropriate to the one congregation would have been unintelligible to the other. But I was entirely wrong in supposing that a non-academic congregation was in some sense less *intelligent* than an under-graduate congregation. On the contrary, I became aware that I was dealing now, perhaps for the first time, with mature adults for whom thinking was no intellectual game but a function of living. They would have no patience with me if I tried to play intellectual games with them. But if I spoke to them of life as they knew it and lived it they would listen; and I soon discovered that in this context I was speaking not only to my intellectual peers but often to my superiors. They understood as well as I did, often better, what I was talking about. They did not want to hear moral platitudes or sentimental anecdotes. They were far too intelligent for that. They wanted real meat and would be satisfied with nothing less. In consequence the sheer *intellectual* demand now being made was greater not less than it had previously been. It was still the big theological questions with which I would be required to grapple; but now I should have to do it twice a Sunday and in a language and imagery for which my university training and chaplaincy experience had given me little aptitude. I found myself intellectually stretched to the limit. I must underline this point. The preacher in the average congregation, town or country, is talking to people who are not stupid. It is *our* intellectual incompetence, not theirs, that is the barrier to communication and understanding.

To meet this challenge the preacher requires all the intellectual capital he can lay his hands on. The amassing of this capital is an important part of his university and college training. Of course he'll go bankrupt if he tries to live for very long off the capital his training has provided. He must constantly be adding to his intellectual reserves as well as drawing from them. But the pressures of the parish ministry are such that if he does not enter that ministry with an adequately stocked mind he is unlikely to find the time or the opportunity to remedy the situation after his ministry has begun. The minister's professional training capital, measured at least by the time he has taken to acquire it, compares favourably with other professional men. The regular graduate course for the ministry of the Church of Scotland consists of not less than six years' study. Even the non-graduate course takes five. Part of that lengthy training is, rightly, non-vocational, designed to widen the student's intellectual and cultural horizons without any direct concern for the job he is going to do. But at least three years of his studies are specifically *theological*. He has to study Old

25

Testament Language and Literature, New Testament Language and Literature, Systematic Theology, Church History and Practical Theology. These theological studies are not simply a continuation of the liberal education which may already have taken him through the Faculty of Arts (though the liberalising influence of these theological studies is often a valued by-product of their main purpose). But the main purpose is, or ought to be, in the fullest sense of the word, vocational. The *raison d'être* of a Christian theological college is to produce men and women who can understand, interpret and proclaim the Christian *kerygma* to the contemporary world. A small though important minority of the men and women so produced will fulfil this kerygmatic task within the universities and colleges themselves, entering upon an academic life and in due course succeeding their own teachers. A further substantial minority will later engage in educational or social work or in specialised ministries of one kind or another. But the majority will be required to proclaim the gospel in a non-academic environment and from a Christian pulpit. It is to equip himself for the intellectual demands of *this* task that the regular student has undergone some six years of university and college training. He is entitled to expect that the intellectual capital he has acquired during these years he will now be able to draw on and use in his daily work, and especially in his preaching.

Disillusionment comes fast. It very soon becomes clear that, however sound the theological currency he was taught to use in his college days, that currency is foreign and unacceptable to those to whom he preaches. Some are courteously prepared to believe that the currency of theological God-talk is valuable for those who live in the exotic territories where it is minted. But even these sympathetic people who believe we have something of value to offer have no way of judging how valuable our foreign currency is or what the rate of exchange is in terms of the coinage of their own language and experience. The disconcerting discovery that he has the wrong kind of money in his pocket is made by the student-preacher on the first occasion on which he tries to use his lecture-notes in preaching. Even before he sees the glazed look on the faces of his listeners he has a suspicion that he is doing the wrong thing. But why is it wrong? What has he been given this intellectual capital for if it is not in some way to help him in his preaching? So he begins again. This time he tries to grapple with the language difficulty, translating as best he can the technical theological and biblical words his teachers used into the plain English of his hearers' vocabulary. But this task proves immensely difficult and even when it is completed the student-preacher has an uneasy suspicion that he is no longer saying what he meant to say to begin with. In the process of translation the real meaning has escaped. In trying to express the big truth his lecturers taught him in the small words his hearers demand, he has turned the truth into a platitude. This time his hearers have at least understood him but are driven to the conclusion that he has nothing of importance to say. The student-preacher very soon reaches a firm conclusion. Lecture notes are not meant to be preached. That, of course, is a very sensible conclusion with which every theological lecturer would agree. But very easily it can lead to another conclusion which is neither sensible nor safe. Disillusioned at the failure of his first attempts to cash the intellectual capital he has been so painfully amassing at college, the young minister can very easily be led to embrace a quite calamitous conclusion—that the intellectual disciplines to which his theological training have accustomed him are irrelevant to the preaching ministry to which he is called. That is not true. But I believe that much more is required to be done within the colleges and within the curriculum to demonstrate *why* that is not true.

This raises the whole question of the relationship between Practical Theology and the other four theological departments within our Scottish theological faculties—Old Testament, New Testament, Systematic Theology and Church History. There are always extraneous pressures at work which if left unchecked would turn the Department of Practical Theology into a department of hints and helps on how to be a good minister. Of course detailed, specific specialist practical guidance in counselling, in teaching methods, in administration, in social work are urgently required just as there is a need for detailed, specific specialist practical guidance on how to conduct a service of worship and how to preach a sermon. Indeed the recognition of this need in all the divinity faculties and colleges in Scotland makes the Warrack Lectures themselves in one sense redundant and anachronistic. But the function of the Practical Theology department is not simply to help to develop the various working skills that a minister needs. Practical theology is also required to integrate and interpret the theological disciplines of the other four departments so as to show their relevance to the minister's vocation, not least to his vocation as a preacher. If such relevance cannot be established then sooner or later the question must be asked 'Why is this being taught?' The theological faculties and colleges are concerned with the vocational training of their students in the fullest meaning of that word, not simply with the continuance of their liberal education. The vocational content of what is being taught cannot, therefore, be ignored. This does not mean in any sense the lowering of academic standards. Other university faculties do not seem to feel that they have sold their intellectual souls because what is being taught to the undergraduate studying for a first degree is in large measure dictated by the practical requirements of the profession the student is to enter, rather than by the requirements of pure research. Otherwise who would be willing to trust his health to a young doctor? But in the training of the young minister the requirements of pure theological enquiry often seem to be given preference over the practical problems which will confront many students as soon as they graduate. So the practical problems are isolated in one part of one department—as if there were a fear that if the theology of the other four departments also became practical they would somehow lose their intellectual integrity. On the contrary, until in some sense all theology is practical theology it lacks integrity—completeness.

Reputable support for this disreputable thesis is not hard to find. Heinrich Ott, Barth's successor in Basel, has written a book called *Theology and Preaching*. By 'theology' he means dogmatic theology rather than the wider sense of the word which I have been using. But I believe the truth of what he has to say is applicable in the wider as well as in the narrower context. Ott writes:

'It may be necessary to affirm that dogmatics is the conscience of preaching and that preaching, again, is the heart and soul of dogmatics. In order to be able to preach at all well, the preacher must engage in dogmatic reflection; while the dogmatic theologian, in

29

order to teach dogma well and truly, must realise that he works with the intention of preaching, and must constantly bear in mind the mission of preaching, even though he himself does not have to mount the pulpit Sunday by Sunday. That preacher who proposed to be nothing other than a preacher and to leave dogmatic thinking to the specialist in dogma would be a bad preacher, a preacher without heart and conscience. And the dogmatist who proposed to be nothing other than a dogmatist and to leave to the pastor the concern with the practical task of church preaching would be a bad church teacher; he again would be a dogmatist without heart and soul and conscience. In former times the theological teachers of the Church were, to a far greater extent than at present, preachers also and conversely (e.g. Luther! Calvin! Zwingli!). This state of affairs reflected the essential truth of the situation. In the years of his Göttingen professorship Karl Barth seriously considered whether he ought not to return to the pastoral office. The separation between the duties of preaching and theological teaching is a purely practical technical division of labour. . . .

Dogmatics is a preaching to preachers, a pastoral charge of those who find themselves in the difficult, extreme, readily assailable position of having themselves to proclaim the Word of God.

It turns its attention to the preacher not with the intention of training him for the fulfilment of his vocation, not with technical means of assistance in the accomplishment of the duties of his calling. This would not be appropriate to the truth of the situation. In such a way it is not possible to be "trained" for the fulfilling of just *this* "calling". Rather dogmatics has to exercise a real preaching and pastoral office, has to bring about a sort of initiation which does not simply impart to the preacher what he must then pass on to his congregation, but which conveys to him the truth, truth by which he himself can live' (*Theology and Preaching*, pages 22–23).

I find all that Ott says here extremely helpful and I want to enlarge on some of the issues that he is raising. Take the last point first. A theological education does not simply impart to the preacher what he must then pass on to his congregation. Its object is 'to bring about a sort of initiation which conveys to (the preacher) the truth by which he himself can live'. Only these theological insights which have penetrated the student's own thought processes and become a part of his own firm conviction will later serve as a source and inspiration for his preaching. Indeed, only this will be remembered. The rest will be forgotten as soon as the requirements of a merciful external examiner allow it.

The initiation of which Ott speaks can, of course, sometimes be a painful and unwelcome experience. The student may have to be exposed to theological climates which he finds entirely uncongenial. But only by such experience can he hope to attain to what Ott calls 'the truth by which he himself can live'. Sometimes his teachers will have to lead him through theological territory which he finds alien and hostile. In the end he may well return to make his home not far distant from where he was before his theological training began. But now he will be a man who has seen the theological world and in consequence he will now see even old familiar things with new eyes. With others, of course, the initiation may take a quite different course. The student may find his theological training an exciting and reassuring experience in which the faith he previously held is confirmed, enriched and

31

articulated. Alternatively, he may find that the faith he previously held has to yield to a new and better faith to which his theological studies have led him. In any of these different ways a student's theological education can convey to him 'the truth by which he himself can live'. But the outcome is not always so happy. Sometimes a student can leave college uncertain whether he has any such intellectual anchor. He has been compelled to abandon the inadequate truth with which he began his course but he has not yet found anything to replace it. Having been led by his teachers into strange and alien territories he knows that he cannot now find the way back to the safe familiar ground he knew before his initiation began; but he no longer knows where he is or where he's going. Sometimes for fear of being so led and lost the student may quite simply refuse to be taught. This points to the need to recognise what Ott calls 'the pastoral office' of theological teaching.

This pastoral office is not an additional extra to be considered only after the exacting academic demands of the curriculum have been met. It is the theological teacher's job to help each student in his care to find 'truth by which he himself can live'. His task is, as Ott says '. . . preaching to preachers, a pastoral charge of those who find themselves in the difficult, extreme and readily assailable position of having themselves to proclaim the Word of God'.

It is interesting to see how far Ott is prepared to go in developing this line of thought. Bultmann and Fuchs have both maintained that theology and preaching are functionally related in such a way as to make the theologian not only the mentor but also the servant of the preacher. But this is not good enough for Ott. Having quoted with disapproval Fuch's modest claim that 'theology is not preaching' Ott goes on: 'No doubt Bultmann—and certainly his pupil Fuchs—sees theology in close connection with preaching. It is there for the sake of preaching. But everything very much depends on how this close connection is understood and defined. For two different things are involved, whether we speak only of a belonging together or whether we speak of a continuity between preaching and theology' (*Theology and Preaching*, pp. 20-21). The issue between Ott and Fuchs is a real and important one but one which for the purpose of our argument need not be pursued. Whether or not there is a continuity between theology and preaching, all parties to the debate are agreed that 'theology is there for the sake of preaching'. The conclusion seems inescapable. A theology which is not seen in some sense to be relevant to preaching is an inadequate theology. If preaching is not, as Ott says, 'the heart and soul of theology' then something is wrong.

But unless this is to lead to gross misunderstanding the other half of what Ott has to say must be equally stressed. Theology is the conscience of preaching. This is so obvious it ought not to need saying. But the temptation for the preacher is always there to preach untheologically or to preach bad theology if by so doing he can be interesting or perhaps even eloquent. It is unlikely that there will be anyone in his congregation who is technically competent to judge the essentially *theological* content of what he is saying. That in itself makes heavy demands on the preacher's integrity. But, more than that, there will be some among his hearers—including some highly intelligent people—who would not care and who might not even notice if his sermon contained no theology at all beyond an occasional reference to God and Christ as his ultimate authority for saying whatever he is saying—even when he is saying no more than 'It's nice to be nice and it's good to be good'. The pressure on him from the majority of his hearers is not that he should be theological but simply that he should be interesting. This is not as frivolous a demand as at first might appear. The word 'interest'—'inter-est'—has overtones of involvement in its derivative meaning that are highly relevant to the preacher's task. Unless he is interesting his congregation he is wasting his breath and their time, however theological the content of what he is saying may be. Of course his object is to be both theological and interesting. In the long run he may well discover that he cannot be interesting unless he is theological for he has nothing else to be interesting about. But in the short run the choice looks rather different. Theological preaching will require that he himself somehow finds the time to continue his own theological education. Not all of us do. Even those of us who have maintained some kind of theological literacy through our pastoral and preaching ministry have often found too much for us the hermeneutic task of translating our own theological convictions into language that will communicate to our hearers on a Sunday and will involve and 'inter-est' them in the same way that we ourselves have been involved, and interested. So rather than become uninteresting we become untheological. Sometimes, indeed, such untheological preaching can succeed splendidly in its declared purpose of holding people's interest—in the same way that a man like Alistair Cooke in his 'Letters from America' can hold his listeners' interest even on the occasions when he is saying little or nothing. It is at such times when we have successfully preached an 'interesting' sermon with a negligible theological content that we need Ott's reminder that theology is the conscience of preaching. I have suffered the painful privilege during all but a few years of my preaching ministry of having at least one member of a theological faculty sitting Sunday by Sunday facing me when I entered my pulpit. Often I've found that theological presence inhibiting, sometimes downright paralysing. But in the end it was a salutary experience though often embarrassing and sometimes humiliating. To have the theologian sitting there while one preaches is a physical reminder that theology is the conscience of preaching. Often for me that has meant having a bad conscience, but a bad conscience is better than none at all. Every preacher, if not in fact then at least in imagination, should see the theologian sitting there in the pews as he preaches, for that is his conscience.

'Preaching is the heart and soul of theology.' 'Theology is the conscience of preaching.' The practical consequences of this mutual recognition of function by theologian and by preacher are obvious and far reaching. The immediate point I am concerned with is limited but important. This way of understanding the interdependence of the work of the academic theologian on the one hand and the working minister on the other should mean that the intellectual energy generated by a student's theological training can be harnessed effectively to his preaching task. At present that energy is often being dissipated almost as soon as the student leaves college with the consequence that the young minister is left to face his preaching ministry intellectually ill-equipped and incompetent. To remedy this situation requires that both the academic theologian and the working minister learn the same lesson. As Ott says: 'Theology is for the sake of preaching'.

2. Preaching and the Will

So far we have been primarily concerned with the intellectual demands of preaching and how best these demands are to be met using the resources at our disposal. But when we preach we appeal not only to the intellect but also to the will and to the emotions of our hearers. I have spoken first and spoken at length about the intellectual demands of preaching because these are the demands which the preacher himself must first meet before he can with integrity appeal to the will or the emotions. But in preaching it is primarily the *will* rather than the intellect or the emotions that he is seeking to involve. Before the will can be engaged the legitimate demands of the intellect must be met. After the will has been engaged the emotional involvement should follow. But the will is the target. Preaching is always primarily preaching for a decision. This decision means not merely the intellectual assent which requires a change of opinion but the moral assent which requires a change of life-style.

Alan Richardson sums up the situation when he writes:

'According to the teaching of the Bible itself, knowledge of the right is the beginning of the knowledge of God; moreover, knowledge of God in this sense is universal, although apart from special revelation men do not recognise it for what it truly is. The sense of obligation to do that which is believed to be right is in fact the pressure of God upon every human life. God is made known to all men, even though they may not have learned to call Him God, as moral demand; and obedience to the behests of conscience is the essential condition of growth in the knowledge of God, just as disobedience to the known moral law is the

36

degrading of the knowledge of God. According to the Bible our knowledge of God is not like our knowledge of electrons or square roots; we know truth about God only by doing it, not by talking or reasoning about it, just as we know love only by loving. Truth in the biblical sense is something to be practised. By engaging actively in the task of setting up justice, of promoting useful ends in society, or of ordering the common life on the basis of one's knowledge of right—this is the way in which the knowledge of God is attained, rather than by reading books upon theology or by reasoning about the First Cause. Theology and reasoning are not in themselves sources of our knowledge of God; they are only the intellectual means by which the truth about God is formulated and its meaning more clearly seen' (*Christian Apologetics*, pp. 124–5).

That puts the intellectual-theological element in our knowledge of God into its proper perspective. More than that, Richardson is arguing that the fact of moral consciousness, the sense of obligation, is itself evidence of a general revelation—'God is made known to all men, even though they may not have learned to call him God, as moral demand'. If this is true then the preacher's task will be to point to the shrine of the Unknown God of moral demand and to say, like Paul at Athens 'What you worship but do not know, this is what I now proclaim' (Acts 17:23).

Brunner's defence of natural theology in his controversy with Barth points in the same direction.

'Let me point out briefly the practical ecclesiastical significance of *theologia naturalis*. The task of the Church is the proclamation of her message. The Church can effect this proclamation in various ways—by preaching, by teaching, by pastoral work, by theology, by personal witness, etc. But wherever the Church proclaims the Word of God in human words, she must choose from amongst human words those that somehow correspond adequately to the divine Word. The objective reason for this correspondence, i.e. for the possibility of speaking of God and of proclaiming his Word at all, is the fact that God has made us in his image. The subjective reason is the revelation of this fact made to us in Jesus Christ. The incarnation is the *criterion of the knowledge* of the divine likeness of man, of its truth and of its profundity. But man's undestroyed formal likeness to God is the *objective possibility* of the revelation of God in his "Word".

The Church could not proclaim her message but for the creaturely relation between the word of man and the Word of God. The fact of the Church's message rests upon this "remnant" of the *imago Dei*. The contents of this message rest upon the restoration of the image of Christ. The Church also is dependent upon the possibility "of speaking to man of God at all". That is the "point of contact": capacity for words and responsibility' (*Natural Theology*, p. 56).

That bears repetition! According to Brunner, the point of contact on which depends the possibility of speaking to man of God at all is our capacity for words and responsibility. Barth of course will have none of this:

'In my experience the best way of dealing with "unbelievers" and modern youth is not to try to bring out their "capacity for revelation", but to treat them quietly, simply (remembering that Christ has died and risen also for them), as if their rejection of "Christianity" was not to be taken seriously.... I have the impression that my sermons reach and "interest" my audiences most when I least rely on anything to "correspond" to the Word of God already "being there", when I least rely on the "possibility" of proclaiming this Word, when I least rely on my ability to "reach" people by my rhetoric, when on the contrary I *allow* my language to be formed and shaped and adapted as much as possible by what the text seems to be saying' (*Natural Theology*, p. 127).

There is a fundamental cleavage of theological opinion here concerning which the preacher has got to make a decision. Are we to search for Brunner's 'point of contact' in the inter-personal experience or moral consciousness of our hearers, or is that a mere dabbling in anthropology and psychology? Are we to try to grapple with the doubts of Christian agnostics by stripping away the incognito of the Unknown God whom already they 'worship but do not know' or are we to treat them 'as if their rejection of Christianity was not to be taken seriously'? Or, to revert to an earlier image, are we to speak of God in the language of the contemporary world (the language of Babylon if you like) or in the language of Biblical theology (the language of Canaan)? The answers given to these basic theological questions will determine not only the content but also the structure and style of one's preaching. To make sense of what follows I must declare my own position. I believe (with Brunner) that there *is* a 'point of contact' for the Gospel which the preacher must search for and recognise in his hearers if the Word of God is to be clearly heard. I believe that that point of contact is to be found primarily, though not exclusively, in inter-personal experience and moral consciousness which I am persuaded are areas of proper concern for the theologian and not just for the anthropologist or psychologist. I believe that the doubts of the Christian agnostic (of whom there are many in the Church's membership including the Church's ministry) are to be taken as seriously as I expect my own doubts to be taken by those who care for me. I believe that Paul's words on Mars Hill 'What you worship but do not know, this is what I now proclaim' is potentially the text of many sermons. I believe that the language of the pulpit must be not only Biblical but also contemporary, the language of Canaan translated into the language of Babylon.

Having made that general confession of faith let me return to Richardson's phrase which opened up these wider issues. 'God is made known to all men, though they may not have learned to call him God, as moral demand.' It is in this sense that I have said that the will rather than the intellect or the emotions is the primary target of preaching. 'Whoever has the will to do the will of God shall know . . .' (John 7:17). 'What must I *do* to be saved?' (Acts 16:30). 'Anything you did for one of my brothers here however humble you did for me', or 'you did not do it for me'—and the difference between doing and not-doing is the difference between eternal life and eternal punishment (Matt. 25:40–45). We simply dare not ignore these passages and countless others like them in the New Testament. But how can we do justice to this kind of 'activism' without involvement in some kind of doctrine of works and a consequent loss of the essential *kerygma* which declares not what man ought to do but what God has done? Can we accept that 'God is made known to us as moral demand' without our preaching becoming mere moralising, or worse still, moral hectoring? I believe that we can and that we must. Theology and Ethics are not two subjects but one. This is not necessarily to deny the value of C. H. Dodd's distinction between *kerygma* and *didache*—though that distinction may have been made rather more rigid than the evidence warrants. Nor does this identification of theology with ethics mean a blurring of the distinction between the human and the divine, between God-talk and Man-talk. For Barth himself ethics is a part of dogmatics and in consequence ethics and dogmatics must be preached together. Tillich agrees:

> 'Today, in spite of the fact that some theological faculties have well-developed departments of Christian ethics, a trend toward taking theological ethics back into the unity of the system can be seen. This trend has been supported by the neo-orthodox movement's rejection of an independent theological ethic. A theology which, like the present system, emphasizes the existential character of theology must follow this trend all the way to its very end. The ethical element is a necessary—and often predominant—element in every theological statement' (*Systematic Theology*, Vol. 1, p. 31).

John Wren Lewis makes the same point very sharply when he writes:

> 'Moral assertions about human interrelationship are not derived "at second hand" from the fact that the Being called "God" just happens to be interested in justice—they are directly and integrally bound up with assertions about God's Being in itself' (*They became Anglicans*, p. 170f).

It appears, then, that theologians variously placed

along the theological spectrum are all agreed on one point: theology and ethics are inseparable. Although the Gospel is primarily concerned not with what we ought to do but with what God has done, it is only through what we ought to do—through our striving *and* our failing—that we come to understand what God has done. If this is true, then ethical talk in preaching need not be merely an apologetic preparation for the main theological thrust of the sermon or, alternatively, the practical application of a theological doctrine already expounded. Ethical talk can indeed fulfil both of these functions and should be allowed to do so. But ethical talk, talk about human relationships, can itself be God-talk, can even be authentically kerygmatic. It is in this sense that John Wren Lewis writes: 'Moral assertions about human interrelationships are not derived "at second-hand" from the fact that a Being called God just happens to be interested in justice—they are directly and integrally bound up with assertions about God's Being in itself'.

My point is simply this: all of us, I think, have a healthy distaste for the kind of moralising and moral hectoring that sometimes characterised preaching of an earlier age. But we are misled if we allow ourselves to forget that Christian preaching is directed primarily toward the listener's will. It is demanding of him a decision and a change of life style. It is questioning his moral assumptions, it is challenging him to do and to be something different from what he is and does. Here ethical language is natural and appropriate. Of course it cannot express itself merely in terms of moral exhortation, for the dynamic that makes this change of life-style (this conversion) possible is not conjured up out of the resources of a man's own will but comes to him from beyond himself—'I, yet not I'. Here, supremely, theology and ethics interpenetrate and ethical talk becomes kerygmatic. Any attempt to draw a rigid line between theology and ethics is to be resisted. Otherwise we get the kind of sermon which is two-thirds a depressing moral analysis of the human situation and then for conclusion adds a theological post-script invoking God to put things right again. And, as neither the ethical talk nor the God-talk says anything to the will the question remains unanswered 'What must I *do* to be saved?' and the Word of God is not heard.

If Richardson is right in saying that 'God is made known to all men as moral demand' then clearly ethical talk in preaching need not be mere moralising but can be genuine practical theology. If Brunner is right in saying that the point of contact on which depends the possibility of speaking to man of God at all is our 'capacity for words *and responsibility*' then ethical talk is an essential instrument in the proclamation of the kerygma. If Wren Lewis is right in saying that 'moral assertions . . . are directly and integrally bound up with assertions about God' then ethical talk can itself be kerygmatic.

The conclusion is clear. In our desire to be kerygmatic, in our fear of moralising we must not ignore or neglect the moral concerns and sensitivities of our hearers for I am persuaded that it is in this area of moral concern that many both within and without the Church meet God and are used by him. Often they meet him incognito but the meeting is none the less real on that account. Among the young, for instance, there is a moral awareness, a moral concern, a questioning and seeking far more radical than anything I remember during my own would-be radical student days. The vast majority of these young people have no patience with

43

what to them is 'mere theology' but their moral concern has about it an evangelical fervour that makes one wonder if they are not sometimes nearer to the Kingdom of God than we are in our churches. If, as Richardson says, 'God is made known to all men as moral demand' that would not be surprising. One thing is certain: it is in ethical rather than in theological terms that contemporary men and women, young and old, are asking the really big questions. In our preaching we must be prepared to speak that language too. Of course that does not mean that we must simply echo in our churches what the world is already saying outside. We must proclaim the Word of God which repeatedly and radically contradicts the word of contemporary man. But we must do so in the language of contemporary man which is the language of moral concern, for God speaks that language too, not just the language of the theologian or the language of Canaan. Above all, in spite of our healthy fear of moralising we must not forget that our preaching is directed primarily towards the *will* and only through the will can adequately reach the intellect. 'He that doeth the will of God shall know. . . .' As Kant realised, 'Practical Reason' is capable of a reach and subtlety that 'Pure Reason' cannot match.

3. Preaching and the Emotions

I've spoken first of the intellect and now of the will as they relate to the preacher's task. It remains to say something on the sensitive subject of the emotions. There is one criticism that many preachers fear even more than the charge of 'mere moralising' and that is the charge of being 'merely emotional'. It goes without saying that emotionalism, the deliberate attempt to manipulate the feelings of one's hearers, is always a dangerous and is sometimes a diabolical enterprise. Hitler mastered the art in the 1930s and turned it into a black magic. Emotional oratory has been suspect ever since, except perhaps in some extreme evangelical Christian circles where its results have not always been reassuring. In consequence those of us who have no natural gift for emotive speech have felt no desire to acquire it and those of us who have that gift have either inhibited it or have used it sparingly with an uneasy conscience. Our hearers in Scotland have not complained, for the Scot is not by nature an emotional extrovert. In consequence our preaching has been directed almost exclusively toward the intellect and the will. We are concerned that our preaching should make some impact on what people think; we are also concerned that our preaching should in some way affect what they do; but how they feel is their business, no one else's, and certainly not ours to tamper with. On the whole I welcome this innate emotional reticence within the Church of Scotland. A distaste for emotionalism is a healthy sign. But the fear of emotionalism like the fear of moralising can become obsessive and inhibiting. Here is a useful corrective from one of my own former teachers, the philosopher John MacMurray:

'What we feel and how we feel is far more important than what we think and how we think. Feeling is the stuff of which our consciousness is made, the atmosphere in which all our thinking and all our conduct is bathed. All the motives which govern and drive our lives are emotional. Love and hate, anger and fear, curiosity and joy are the springs of all that is most noble and most detestable in the history of men and nations. Thought may construct the machinery of civilisation, but it is feeling that drives the machine; and the more powerful the machine is, the more dangerous it is if the feelings which drive it are at fault. Feeling is more important than thought.

Now it is the tradition of our society that this is not true. We are inclined to think of feeling as something a little ignominious, something that ought to be subordinated to reason and treated as blind and chaotic, in need of the bridle and the whip. I am convinced that this is a mistake. It is in the hands of feeling, not of thought, that the government of life should rest. And in this I have the teaching of the founder of Christianity on my side, for he wished to make love—an emotion, not an idea—the basis of the good life' (*Freedom in the Modern World*, p. 146).

Perhaps the case is overstated: 'Feeling is more important than thought' may be deliberately provocative and few of us would accept that *agape* is purely emotional. But the central thrust of the argument is powerful and is to be taken seriously not least in our emotion-shy presbyterian pulpits. According to MacMurray, feeling like thought can be real or unreal, rational or irrational. 'When we feel in an unreal way,' he says, 'our feelings are turned in upon themselves. We enjoy or dislike our feelings, not the object or person who arouses them in us. When we feel in a real way, it is the object or the person that we realise and appreciate' (op. cit. p. 153). So in our preaching we must constantly be on our guard against the kind of emotionalism in which 'our feelings are turned in upon themselves' for to turn in upon ourselves is to turn away from God. But if God in Christ is present in our preaching we must expect some response not only of the

46

intellect and of the will but of the emotions as well. This is of critical importance theologically. Intellect and will alone may hear the Law preached but not the Gospel. The intellect may accept the truth of what is said and the will may strive to act upon it; but until the emotions assent to the intellect, the will will labour and, even if the Gospel is preached, only the Law will be heard. You can see this happening in our churches when you look at a sea of impassive faces. MacMurray is saying the same thing in a totally different context:

'We *can* think that something is worth while doing and do it because we think it is worth while, even when our desires and feelings would prevent us from doing it, though even then it is only with the help of a feeling—a feeling of self-respect or reverence for the ideas which guide our judgment. We call that doing our duty because it is our duty. There are occasions when that is necessary; but if it is necessary there is something wrong somewhere. We only do things because they are our duty when we think that something is worth while doing without feeling that it is worth while. And in that case either our feeling is wrong or our thought is wrong. I want to underline the statement that *our thought may be wrong, and our feeling may be right.* In matters of what is good and bad, feeling is the proper guide; and when we fall back on rules, we are really falling back upon a traditional feeling—the feelings of other people, in fact, because we cannot trust our own. But in that case, the sooner we train ourselves to feel properly, the better' (op. cit. pp. 147–148).

Unless there is some measure of emotional involvement on the part of the preacher and on the part of his hearers the *kerygma* cannot be heard in its fullness for the *kerygma* speaks to the whole man, emotion and all, and simply does not make sense to the intellect and the will alone. The intellect and the will between them can understand the Law: 'We *can* think that something is worth while doing and do it ... even when our desires and feelings would prevent us' but that is the bondage of life under the Law, justification by works. The spontaneity of Christian freedom, of grace, of justification by faith, the *kerygma* itself, is not primarily thought or willed but felt. Only after we have felt it, can we think about it and act upon it. 'We may think that Milton's *Paradise Lost* is a fine poem', says MacMurray, 'and not feel that it is anything but tedious and boring. In that case we do not appreciate it and it is merely dishonest to pretend that we do. It is the things that we really feel, not think worth while, that are worth while *for us* and it is no use trying to substitute our idea for our feeling. Our opinion that things are worth while cannot make them worth while for us if our feelings obstinately refuse to agree' (op. cit. p. 148). Many of us have preached many *Paradise Lost* sermons—thought to be good but felt to be tedious and boring. Then even if we succeed in carrying some kind of intellectual conviction with our hearers and that conviction becomes the spring of good action it will be the Law only that has been heard, however kerygmatic our language. For simply to repeat the kerygmatic formulae, whether in the language of preaching or in the language of the liturgy, can be as arid a legalism as any that Paul knew; what MacMurray calls a 'falling back upon a traditional feeling—the feelings of other people—because we cannot trust our own'. That would seem to me to be fair comment on much of our preaching. Perhaps this is one reason why many of us are so suspicious of emotion in preaching—because we

48

cannot trust our own. 'In that case,' as MacMurray says, 'the sooner we train ourselves to feel properly the better'.

One essential fact must be recognised by the preacher. The truth of the Faith is something that is felt rather than thought by many deeply committed Christian people. MacMurray would say this is a good thing since for him 'What we feel and how we feel is far more important than what we think and how we think'. But whether it is a good thing or not, it remains a fact that many in our congregation who think unreliably about their faith feel authentically about it. This, I believe, is true even in our emotionally reticent Church of Scotland tradition. Felt truths are not to be despised. 'Our thoughts may be wrong and our feeling may be right.' Of course our feeling must constantly be disciplined, examined and questioned by our thought to ensure that it is authentic feeling—in other words that it is a response to the real world and not just sentimentalism which is emotion turned in upon itself. This intellectual discipline is part of the function of preaching. But having distinguished authentic from unauthentic feeling the preacher can then go on to use authentic feeling for cognitive purposes, as a means towards attaining knowledge, including real knowledge of God; that is contained in the Christian Gospel and nowhere else; but when felt truth and the *kerygma* are brought together in preaching, authentic feeling is the catalyst that releases the latent energy of the Word. Sometimes we call this the work of the Spirit.

Once again there are important practical conclusions to be drawn by the preacher. If we are to communicate with our hearers we must try to understand not only what they think but what they feel. We must be concerned not only that they and we think clearly about our Faith but that they and we feel authentically about it as well. 'The sooner we train ourselves to feel properly the better', says MacMurray. This of course concerns the whole ethos of worship and its liturgical structure. But it concerns preaching too. We must not be afraid to talk about how people feel. I know very well the dangers inherent in what I'm saying. I'm not for a moment advocating the kind of subjective introspective preaching which merely invites people to accept that their emotional life is in a mess, offers some hints and tips on how to tidy it up a bit, and then says that this is really all that Jesus was saying once you cut through all the theological clap-trap. I am most certainly not suggesting that the preacher should abandon his profession as a theologian and declare himself instead an amateur psychologist, though it is not without significance that the psychologist and psychiatrist have taken over so many of the pastoral functions of the minister or priest. I am fully aware of the dangers of introspection as a source of theological insight and I fully accept that such introspection can turn a man in on himself and therefore away from God. But accepting all that, I am still persuaded that suspicion of introspection, fear of talking about how people feel, has become for some of us as obsessive as has our fear of moralising and of emotionalism. I do not mean that introspection will itself disclose any of the essential elements of the Christian Gospel; but I *do* mean that introspection can often prove the catalyst necessary to release the latent energy which must be released from the essential elements of the *kerygma* before the chemistry of salvation can be effective. The doctrine of grace is often felt to be true before it is understood to be true. I would go further; the doctrine of grace cannot be understood to be true until it is felt to be true. If I preach on Grace I am asking a man to understand something that has already happened to him, the initiative that God has already taken toward him. What has already happened to him, what he has already felt or is capable of feeling I am asking him to understand in terms of the life and death and resurrection of Jesus. But the proclamation of the life and death and resurrection of Jesus is for him irrelevant until it becomes enmeshed in what he is and does *and feels*. We must not be afraid to talk about how people feel. We must resist the emotional prudery which so much of our intellectual training and pseudo-scientific culture has persuaded us to accept. We must listen to the young, many of whom again have got the message before us—'feeling is more important than thinking'. Of course that is a dangerous doctrine open to abuse and we must regret the dependence of some young people on drugs and on experimentation with sex, as a means of enlarging their emotional experience. But we cannot ignore the implications of the fact that a not insignificant and increasing number of them are turning to *religion* as the only means through which they can find emotional fulfilment; but often not the religion offered by our westernised middle-class institutionalised Christianity with all its emotional hang-ups; but to the emotionally exuberant sects or to the religions of the east which take the emotional life seriously and seek to understand and enlarge it.

4. The Language of Canaan and the Language of Babylon

I have been arguing that the majority of people today are asking the big questions, not, as in past centuries, in

51

the language of theology but in the language of ethics and psychology. We believe that these questions can only be answered theologically. But before people will listen to our theological answers they must be satisfied that we have understood the questions *they* are asking. Much of our preaching gives the appearance of offering painstaking answers to questions that *nobody* is asking. It will not do to reply that we must make people ask the *right* questions, must give them the answer 'whether they will hear or whether they will forbear' (Ez. 2:5) and then leave the rest to God. A foreign missionary must learn to speak the language of those to whom he preaches and if he does not he cannot rely on God to offer any Pentecostal miracles of simultaneous translation to bale him out. We are called to 'sing the Lord's song in a foreign land'. We must *start* by speaking the language of the land in which we find ourselves. We live in Babylon not Canaan and the language of Babylon today when it is talking seriously about human existence is primarily the language of ethics and psychology. We must not be afraid to speak that language or feel that our Gospel is necessarily tainted by being translated into the common tongue. Like every good missionary we must be alert to recognise and welcome those signs in contemporary culture and experience which prove that Christ has been here before us. We must constantly be looking for the shrines, some of them noble ones, that men have built and dedicated 'to an unknown God' and with Paul we must say 'what you worship but do not know—this is what I now proclaim'. This is what I mean by preaching in the language of Babylon. We must start with where people are, from the questions they are asking, using the language they are speaking. The Christian preacher who refuses to speak that language because it is the language of Babylon not the language of Canaan, because it does not express itself in Biblical and theological terms, will simply not be listened to, not because people are hostile to him—many of them *feel* that what he stands for is very important—but because he is speaking in a foreign language of which they understand little or nothing.

I do not mean by that that the preacher must abandon the language of Canaan, must avoid using great Biblical words—like grace, sin, atonement, covenant, redemption—simply because these words are no longer used in common speech, or, if used are used in a misleading sense. On the contrary, one main function of preaching should be the reinstatement of these words, their recovery from the limbo of pietistic meaninglessness into which they have fallen for many of our contemporaries. But this can only be done by trying to translate them as best we may into the language of the common speech and experience of those who listen to us. Of course such translation is difficult and is always in some measure inadequate. But it must be attempted. There is no primitive magic in the sound of these words and a sermon does not become Biblical and kerygmatic merely by their repeated use. They must be set again and again not only within their historical context in the Old and New Testaments (vitally important though that is) but also within the context of real-life situations that are immediately recognisable and familiar to our hearers, so that they become not merely relevant but dynamic *there*. This tension between honest historical exegesis on the one hand and relevant contemporary commentary on the other is really just another aspect of the tension between the language of Canaan and the language of Babylon. It is a fruitful tension of which the preacher should be

53

constantly aware.

William Nicholls expounding 'The New Herm-eneutic' in his *Guide to Modern Theology* has a passage which illustrates the point I am trying to make.

'If the original contentions of the [New Testament] writer are to be understood today, they must be reinter-preted, so that the writer will say what he would have wished to say in our own culture and time.

Every reader of the New Testament engages in inter-pretation, but many do so unconsciously. The naive reader may fail to realise what must be involved if his interpretation is to succeed. He must decide first of all what the words meant for the first-century men who wrote and first read them. Only when he has thus discovered, so far as is possible, the original meaning of the text can he go on to the second part of the task, and attempt to render the same meaning in contemporary terms. Without the resources of scholarship, it is unlikely that either task can be satisfactorily dis-charged. The first depends on a knowledge of the litera-ture, social customs and philosophical outlook of the ancient world, which together provide the context for the thought of the New Testament writers. The second depends on a correct analysis of contemporary culture and *Existenz,* in which personal judgment must necessarily be involved. The common reader usually concentrates, whether he is aware of it or not, on the second task. He makes the biblical writers mean what he thinks it would be appropriate for them to say today, without controlling this by proper exegesis of what they did in fact say to the men of their own time. He fails to grasp the first-century meaning of the text; if in addition he is a conservative, and wishes to reject a twentieth-century one, he is most likely to end with one appropriate to the eighteenth century.

To ignore the problem of communication between cultures is therefore not to escape it but to become its victim. If we assign to the New Testament a meaning it did not have for its first readers, and can have for only a minority of present-day ones, we have failed to bring its message to the life which the believer claims it possesses for all men in every culture. The group of theologians principally associated with the hermeneutic task considers it the duty of the theologian to work in the service of the proclamation of the Gospel to twentieth-century man by performing this double act of translation, or exegesis and commentary, and by making it as truthful as possible. It can only be this if it is as faithful as present-day resources allow both to the original meaning of the text and to the meanings which are possible within our present culture' (*Pelican Guide to Modern Theology*, pp. 320–321).

Out of the tension between 'the original meaning of the text' on the one hand and 'the meanings which are possible within our present culture' on the other is generated the dynamic that makes preaching possible. 'The original meaning of the text' must be honestly sought by the preacher before he can legitimately use it to discover 'possible meanings within our present culture'. That is why the technical academic training he has received in Biblical Criticism must never be allowed to become irrelevant to his homiletic task. He need not insist on telling his congregation all the books he has read and all the alternative interpretations he has considered. He did not read these books simply to pass on to his congregation in digest form the bits that have caught his fancy. Rather, the critical apparatus of Biblical scholarship has been given to him to establish what Ott calls 'the truth by which he himself can live'. He must live and preach in the faith that the closer he comes to an understanding of the original meaning of the text of the Bible the closer he comes to the Word of God. That is a big act of faith and it is by no means self-evident that it is justified. But if we accept (as I do) that the Word of God is contained in the Scriptures of the Old and New Testaments then we must accept this also. Unless the primary authority for what we are saying is Biblical, and therefore ultimately dependent on the original meaning of the text, we are not preaching, we are simply expressing an opinion.

But that is only half the truth. A true exposition of the original meaning of the text offers no guarantee that the Word of God has been preached. The *kerygma* is not heard unless 'the meanings which are possible within our present culture' are also realised: this is what demonstrates the text of the Bible to be the Word of God—its capacity to speak to men and women in our present culture. And by 'present culture' I mean simply how people think, act and feel now. Until the text of the Bible has been shown to be relevant and potent in the immediate social and personal concerns of contemporary life, it has not become the Word of God, however faithful the textual exegesis. And as we have seen that these contemporary concerns are expressed in our present culture not primarily in theological but in ethical and psychological terms, the preacher must be prepared to speak in these terms if 'the meanings which are possible within our present culture' are to be recognised. Yet 'the original meaning of the text' must remain the controlling factor. Hence the tension. The preacher is pulled in two different directions at once, which is never comfortable. But to try to escape the discomfort is disastrous, for out of this tension is generated the power which alone makes preaching possible. Every sermon is stretched like a bowstring between the text of the Bible on the one hand and the problems of contemporary human life on the other. If the string is insecurely tethered to either end, the bow is useless. It is a wise precaution for every preacher to pay special attention to the end of the string which for him is the less securely tethered. The other end will look after itself, meantime at least.

5. What is said and what is heard

One further matter remains to be discussed before my argument ends. It stems from the fact that preaching uses as its essential instrument the spoken word. Whenever words are spoken and heard some kind of personal relationship, however superficial, is established between the speaker and the hearer. Within this relationship words have an extra dimension which the printed page does not contain. This remains true even when the relationship between the speaker and the hearer is wholly impersonal in every respect except one, that the spoken word has passed between them. It can even survive the extreme depersonalisation implicit in all mass media of communication. The successful radio or television performer, whether he is an entertainer or a more serious communicator, invariably owes his success not to the fact that he is intrinsically funnier or better informed than others in the same field but to his capacity to create the illusion of a real personal relationship between himself and his audience. It is this that makes his jokes sound funnier or his facts more interesting and authoritative than those of other men. Of course it is only an illusory relationship that is created between performer and audience, but it is a powerful illusion that can sometimes make a talking head on television or a disembodied voice on radio seem more real than people we know. The spoken word has this intrinsic power. Whenever words are spoken and heard some kind of personal relationship, real or illusory, is established and what is heard will depend not just on what is said but on the nature of that personal relationship.

When we preach, what is heard depends not only on what is said but on the nature of the personal relationship between preacher and congregation. It is a sound instinct that requires that the office of preacher and pastor should be combined in one man. Preaching and pastoral care sometimes, indeed, seem to compete with one another for a minister's time and attention. Moreover, some men are more gifted in the one ministry than in the other and it is natural that in a period of increasing specialisation some men feel they ought to be allowed to concentrate on one job and do that really well. Preaching divorced from pastoral concern is blind. It neither knows what it is talking about nor to whom it is talking. It does not know what it is talking about because it does not know the real-life situations of those who listen, within which alone the text of the Bible can become the Word of God. But, more serious, it is blind because it does not know to whom it speaks. It is significant that many congregations will not turn out as their minister expects them to for distinguished visiting preachers. They prefer their own man, not because what he says is better than what is said by the distinguished visitor (it is often much worse); but because what he says is said within a special relationship of pastor and people. By the same token many ministers find, as I did, that there is only one pulpit that they can really preach from and that is their own. What is said there may often be less than adequate, but what is heard is more than what is said because it is heard within a special personal relationship. I'm speaking now from personal knowledge but also from a sense of personal failure. The congregation I ministered to till recently numbered 2700—far too big for one man and I didn't really know half of them. I have clear evidence that those for whom my preaching meant something were those who knew me as a pastor or those who even knew of me as a pastor. Those whom I did not know, who knew me only as a preacher and who supposed that I spent my week preparing Sunday's sermon, can only have thought of me as some kind of performer, probably a bad one. And if I had spoken 'with the tongues of men and of angels' it would have made no difference so long as I spoke within that impersonal relationship. No man can establish intimate personal relationships with every member of his congregation, especially if it is a very large one. But if his hearers know him, or even know of him, as a good pastor then they will hear more than he says and the Word of God will have been preached. Sometimes our failure as preachers is only our failure as pastors in disguise. Sometimes the Word of God is heard when a good pastor preaches a bad sermon, because what is heard depends not only on what is said but on the nature of the relationship between speaker and hearer. If our preaching fails, one possible reason for that failure may be the inadequacy of that relationship rather than the inadequacy of what we have said.

But this is only to scratch the surface of the matter. If what is heard depends not just on what is said but on the relationship between the speaker and the hearer, and if in preaching God speaks, then the whole problem of communication takes on a new dimension. The hearing of the Word of God will depend not primarily on the relationship between preacher and congregation but on the relationship of preacher and congregation with God. If we could assume that we were preaching to people who were regularly practising the tried and proved traditional forms of devotion and piety, private prayer and Bible study, then our task would be immeasurably easier than it is. But many of our listeners do not pray regularly, and study their Bibles hardly at all. We can and we must encourage the recovery of personal devotion in these traditional forms. Some of us could well start by examining our own devotional life. We spend much time preparing our prayers for public worship, often far less time saying our prayers of private devotion. We spend much time searching the Scriptures for sermons often forgetting that until the Bible has spoken its personal word to us in our situation we cannot preach it to others in theirs. It is therefore a matter of urgency that we should seek to recover both for ourselves and for our hearers the practice of prayer and Bible study—and this not only as a public act in the Church but as a private act in the home. Otherwise the personal relationship of preacher and congregation with God which alone makes the hearing of the Word possible will be seriously impoverished.

But a right relationship of preacher and congregation with God is not solely to be achieved by a re-establishment of traditional forms of devotion and piety. Nor will any good come of our pretending that we are all practising these traditional forms when we know that many of us are not. Rather—if the argument so far is accepted—a right relationship with God will be established through the realisation that the whole of life and experience—intellectual, moral and emotional—is the field of God's self-disclosure. So in our intellectual, moral and emotional involvement with other people we are already involved with God, even those of us whose devotional life in traditional terms is woefully inadequate. Our relationship with others and our relationship with God are inextricably interwoven. 'Everyone who loves is a child of God and knows God, but the unloving know nothing of God' (1 John 4: 7 and 8). The implications of that text for the preacher are clear. Where there is caring there is knowledge of God, where there is not there is none. Only within a personal caring relationship can we communicate in depth with one another and God with us. This is why the functions of preacher and pastor belong together. This is why every sermon is a bowstring held in tension between the text of the Bible on the one hand and the problems of human life on the other. This is why the whole of human experience must be recognised and be used by the preacher as the field of God's self-disclosure—since intellect, will and emotion are all involved in caring.

6. Summary and Transition

I have been arguing that theology is for preaching. I believe that has been shown to be true in several quite different senses. Theology is for preaching in the sense that the great theologians of our own day are 'for' preaching and see it as quite literally the beginning and the end of theology. Theology is for preaching in the sense that what is taught in our theological colleges must be seen to be relevant to the preacher's task by fulfilling its pastoral functions of leading him to the

61

truth by which he himself can live. Theology is for preaching in the sense that theology is the conscience of preaching. Theology is for preaching in a very special sense once it is recognised that theology is not simply an intellectual exercise, that the intellect is not the only or even the primary channel of God's self-disclosure, but that God speaks to men through the will and the emotions as well. Theology is for preaching in the quite specific hermeneutic sense that its task is to translate the words of the Bible into the Word of God for our own time. Theology is for preaching in the sense that the preached word becomes the Word of God within a special relationship of person to person and of persons to God, a relationship which alone makes theology and preaching possible. That in telegraphic summary is the ground we have covered so far.

In the space that remains I want to try to show how these theological considerations take form and substance in the practical task of sermon preparation. In the next section I shall therefore outline some general principles of sermon construction which I believe to be of value. Then in the final section I shall try to illustrate from actual sermon material how these practical principles can combine with the theological guidelines already laid down to create and fashion the stuff of preaching. I would wish to stress that what follows is not offered as a model of how it ought to be done but simply as a description of how one man very inadequately does it. As in preaching itself, so in talking about preaching, the listener can receive the truth for himself not only through his assent to what is said but through his dissent as well. So when I speak in the imperative the only person to whom I am being imperious is myself, for I am the only person to whom I can speak with assurance. If there is valid counsel for others here it will be non-directive counselling—an invitation from one preacher to his colleagues to compare notes so that by agreement with what is said or by reaction against it each may find the answer to his own problems. There are no general rules. What is good counsel for one man is bad counsel for another. What is good counsel for one man in one place at one time is bad counsel even for the same man in a different place at a different time. Having thus covered my tracks against the charge of dogmatism I shall now allow myself in the pages which follow the luxury of speaking as dogmatically as I please!

3
GUIDELINES:
FOLLY DESCRIBED

1. Unity

Every sermon should be ruthlessly unitary in its theme. 'This is the first and great commandment!' When as a student or probationer one is asked to preach only occasionally it is natural to be a little profligate with one's material. When one is required to preach twice a Sunday one becomes more miserly. But it is a mistake to think that the miser is a less effective preacher than the profligate. When a man plots out a small area of a field and digs deep there he is more likely to find hidden treasure than the man who scrapes with a rake the surface of the whole field. Heinrich Ott, who certainly cannot be charged with theological irresponsibility, writes as follows:

> 'I can never preach about everything; it is not right that I should wish to express "everything". We preach in antithesis: sometimes of the judgment, sometimes of the mercy of God, sometimes of justification, sometimes of sanctification. As preachers, we testify to God's honour and glory in a one-sided way, concentrating our attention on the particular aspect which the text suggests to our minds. If it is given us to testify truly in this way, then God is present as the one, eternal, unchanging being, and the particular sermon enfolds, in all its particularity, the whole . . .

The particular sermon is like the smaller part of the iceberg that is visible above the water; the rest, the totality of the kergyma committed to the Church, floats sustainingly beneath the surface of the water. This symbolises dogmatic reflection on the wholeness of the doctrine which sustains and enfolds the particular sermon. We ought to feel uneasy about those critics who declare that they "miss" references to the "cross" or the "resurrection" in some particular sermon. As though it were the duty of the preacher to be always expressing everything! As though it were his duty at any and every cost to push into his sermon every article of Christian doctrine! For where the cross is truly proclaimed, then the resurrection is proclaimed also; where God's grace is preached, so is also His judgment; where justification is truly declared, so also is the process of sanctification' (*Theology and Preaching*, pp. 26–27).

It should be possible in one simple sentence, without relative clauses, to state what the subject matter of a sermon is. Anything in the sermon which cannot be justified as relevant to that central theme should be ruthlessly discarded. The chances are that the material discarded contains seminal ideas for other sermons which is all the more reason for refusing to waste them now on a mere digression. Next week will be here soon enough and this week's digression may provide the main thrust for next week's theme. Meantime everything depends on finding a theme which is strong enough to allow development in depth without digression.

An article on the composer Haydn in Grove's *Dictionary of Music* contains an interesting passage. The contributor (C. F. Pohl) writes:

'When an idea struck [Haydn] he sketched it out in a

few notes and figures: this would be his morning's work; in the afternoon he would enlarge this sketch, elaborating it according to rule but taking pains to preserve the unity of the idea. "That is where so many young composers fail," he says; "they string together a number of fragments; they break off almost as soon as they have begun; and so at the end, the listener carries away no definite impression" ' (Grove's *Dictionary of Music*, Vol. 1, p. 718).

Pohl's description of Haydn's method of work seems to me to be an admirable model for the preacher to follow. A morning is well spent producing 'a few notes' if one can see latent in those few notes a whole sermon. The few notes often require to be worked over again and again until they can be seen to imply all that the sermon is going to contain. Then and only then is the preacher in a position to decide what he will first actually *say* to his congregation, for he cannot know where to begin until he knows where he is going to end. It is simply no use writing an elegant introductory paragraph to a non-existent theme in the hope that by the time it is written some theme will have emerged. At the best the next paragraph may emerge, it in turn may suggest another paragraph and so on until sufficient paper has been covered to give the preacher enough courage to mount his pulpit steps. But what he will have produced will not be a sermon but merely an exercise in free association. There will be no clearly stated theme, no common point of reference, no home key, no development, only a medley of ideas linked by nothing stronger than the fact that the preacher in his study thought of them one after the other. Here Haydn's criticism of young composers is seen to be equally relevant to some young preachers—and others not so young: 'They string together a number of fragments; they break off almost as soon as they have begun; and so, at the end, the listener carries away no definite impression.'

In any kind of composition it is form that gives unity and unity that holds attention. A composer of music will become boring to himself and to his listeners if he always writes in the same form, but *some* form there must always be. He need not insist on telling his listeners about the form he has chosen—'firstly, secondly, thirdly brethren'—for if the form is implicit in his material it will be sensed by the listener even though it is not specifically identified. Few concert-goers could analyse the structure of the music they have heard yet their appreciation of the music depends on that structure and on the feeling of unity it creates. At the same time if the form is not implicit in the subject matter, no imposed formal structure will better the case. In other words, everything depends on the care with which we choose the few notes out of which the sermon is to grow. As Pohl says of Haydn 'when an idea struck him he sketched it out in a few notes. . . . This would be his morning's work'. A few dozen seminal words rightly chosen are better reward for a morning's work than many pages of foolscap ill-conceived.

2. Exegesis of the Text and 'Exegesis of Life'

The preacher, having chosen his theme and 'sketched it out in a few notes', can then continue to follow Haydn's excellent example by 'enlarging the sketch, elaborating it according to rule'. The rules of course will vary and will be determined by the form chosen. But certain patterns recur. Textual exegesis is one essential way in which the preacher will enlarge and elaborate his theme. He may do so by setting the text in its context, explaining what it meant to the man who wrote it and to those who first read it. His exegesis must not be biased and he must not allow his text to become a mere pretext for what he was intending to say in any case. On the other hand his exegesis must not appear to his hearers to be a matter of merely academic or antiquarian interest. Historical and cultural background may indeed be of great value in establishing the context of the passage under discussion and the preacher himself should be thoroughly informed in this regard. But he should not feel that it is his duty to pass on to the congregation, even in digest form, all the information that he himself has acquired, all the alternative interpretations that he himself has considered and rejected. Theology is indeed the conscience of preaching but the preacher is not always required to parade his conscience in public. Of all the exegetical material available to him he should use that alone which is relevant to his theme. Don't misunderstand me. If this means distorting the exegesis then he has chosen the wrong text or the wrong theme or both and had better start again. Honest exegesis is essential. Sometimes it may be extensive, sometimes it may be very brief. If it is extensive, what is said must be seen to be necessary and relevant to the main contemporary thrust of the sermon. If it is brief it need not be perfunctory or superficial so long as the preacher himself has done his own homework thoroughly and with intellectual integrity. Brief or extensive, at some point this exegetical 'enlargement and elaboration' of the text should appear. But it should not be discursive in the way in which the Biblical commentaries on which it is based are themselves necessarily discursive.

In other words—following Haydn's example again—in our exegetical 'enlarging and elaborating according to rule' we must always be 'taking pains to preserve the unity of the idea'.

In the same way and with the same care for unity the preacher will enlarge and elaborate his theme as he finds it, not only in the pages of the Bible, but in the experience of contemporary life which he shares with his hearers; for God's self-disclosure is made not only in the pages of the Bible but in contemporary life and experience as well. The preacher's task is therefore not simply to persuade his hearers that there is an analogy between some situation in the Bible and our situation today, a similarity between the kind of people we find in the Bible and the kind of people we are today and that in consequence we can infer that what God once said to other people in other times is still, in some way, relevant to us in our time. The preacher's task is to proclaim that God through Christ is speaking his Word to us now, not only through the words of the Bible but in the experience of contemporary life which we share together.

If we take any significant element in human life and seek to understand it in depth, not merely with the intellect, but with the will and the emotions as well, we must expect to find the Word incarnate there—the Risen Christ there. Of course, unless our Biblical exegesis and theology are sound we will not recognise Christ in contemporary experience even if we meet him there. That is why, as Barth says, the preacher must always stand 'between Scylla and Charybdis—the Bible on the one hand, the problem of human life on the other'; or, as William Nicolls puts it, between 'the original meaning of the text' on the one hand and 'the meanings possible in our present culture' on the other.

Certainly the Bible and the original meaning of the text have logical and theological precedence. But when the preacher speaks of contemporary life and experience, he is not merely talking of something to which the Word of God is relevant but of something in which the Word of God is already implicit. This has been the main thrust of my theological argument. Thus when the preacher develops his theme in secular and contemporary language and imagery he is not just making a concession to secular contemporary men and women, showing that he understands their world and can talk their language before he invites them to enter his quite different theological world with its quite different vocabulary. The use of such secular contemporary language and imagery is part of his exegetical and hermeneutic task without which the Word cannot be heard.

So the preacher will enlarge and elaborate his theme not only through an exegesis of the Biblical text but through an exegesis of contemporary life and experience as well. These two kinds of exegesis are complementary. Biblical exegesis requires an exegesis of contemporary life and experience to show its relevance. An exegesis of life and experience requires a Biblical exegesis to show its theological content. But each only shows what is there already in the other. A study of contemporary life and experience in depth reveals that the Bible has already plumbed these depths. A study of the Bible reveals the theological content already implicit in contemporary life and experience.

Thus far I have been prepared to be dogmatic. First, strict unity of theme is essential for reasons at once theological, psychological and practical. Second, every theme requires to be developed in two ways: by Biblical exegesis on the one hand and by an exegesis of life and experience on the other. I believe these guide lines to be necessary and reliable, if not for all of us all of the time, at least for most of us most of the time. The same practical conclusions can, of course, be reached from theological premises radically different from those I have argued. Concerning the theology I am open to persuasion. Concerning the practical conclusions so far reached I am unrepentantly dogmatic. From now on, however (as Paul said in a rather different context!), 'I have no command of the Lord but I give my opinion' (1 Cor. 7:25 RSV).

3. From the Known to the Unknown

The development of the theme should move from the known to the unknown, from the truth already accepted to the fuller truth to which the sermon is pointing. In an earlier chapter I have defended the theological propriety of this procedure. Often it will mean beginning with an exegesis of life rather than with an exegesis of the text. The preacher states his theme in terms of some experience which he knows to be shared by himself and his hearers. It may be a specific event, a common emotion, a shared interest, or even something as seemingly ephemeral and trivial as a current catch phrase, or a familiar television programme. Later, when he comes to his Biblical exegesis, he will be required to look—as the hermeneutic theologians remind us—not only for the original meaning of the text but also for the meanings possible within our present culture. The effectiveness of that later Biblical exegesis will depend on how effectively the theme has already been stated in terms of that present culture—and in this context I mean by 'culture' simply how ordinary people think, act and feel. Most of us most of the time think, act and feel superficially and it is at this superficial level that the preacher is often required to start. Having made common ground with his hearers (and without condescension—for many of us who preach live as superficially as the next man) the preacher can then begin an exploration into the depths concealed below the superficiality. At this stage intellect, will and emotion may all become involved—how people think, act and feel—and from this chemistry the real substance of the theme should begin to emerge. The listener should feel that although he has passed from the obvious to the significant—from the natural to the numinous—it is still the world he knows that is being talked about. Francis Thompson's poem *The Kingdom of God* is sub-titled 'In no strange land'. It contains these familiar lines:

> 'The angels keep their ancient places
> Turn but a stone and start a wing'

No preacher is without a theme until he can say with honesty that he has left no stone unturned!

At this point however the exegesis of life may be met by the exegesis of the text and so the listener should be led from the known to the unknown, from the truth already accepted to the fuller truth to which the sermon is pointing. Often the exegesis of the text will prove the critical turning point in the sermon. To the exegesis of life already given it will be responding with an emphatic 'yes, but . . .!' It will say 'yes' and will want to say 'yes' to theological truths revealed in non-theological terms by the exegesis of life. But our exegesis of life, our knowledge of what God is doing in us and our world, is only made possible through our

73

exegesis of the Bible, through our prior knowledge of what God has done in Christ. This is why our Biblical exegesis is nearly always in tension with our exegesis of life. It is the same God who is revealing himself in life and in the Bible. *Yes! But* in life we see him revealed through sinful human nature, in the Bible we see him revealed through the sinless Son of God. Every sermon must contain an exegesis of life to enable the hearer to start where he is with the world he knows and so to see the relevance of the Gospel that is being preached to him. But the substance of that Gospel can only be established through an exegesis of the Bible. Otherwise (to return to Francis Thompson's imagery) however many angel wings we may cause to flutter we shall never see

'. . . Jacob's ladder
Pitched between Heaven and Charing Cross'

That, after all, is what preaching is about—showing people the ladder between Heaven and Charing Cross. We must start at Charing Cross, but we must not be content to stay there.

4. Levels of Meaning

I have said that the preacher should move from the known to the unknown, from the truth already accepted to the fuller truth to which the sermon is pointing, from the superficial to the more profound. But this is an over-simplification. In any congregation the capacity for understanding varies widely from person to person as does the mode of understanding. Intellect, will and emotion are all involved but in differing degrees. Some

74

whose intellectual capacities are limited have a moral strength and an emotional maturity which enables them to grasp the meaning of the *kerygma* non-intellectually, yet far more securely than those who are intellectually sophisticated but morally and emotionally immature. Others, on the other hand, find that the will and the emotions cannot become fully involved until first the intellect has been satisfied. In this way the mode of understanding varies. But so also does the capacity for understanding. Some are already far further along the Christian road—intellectually or non-intellectually—than the preacher himself; some have barely started along that road. Some are young, some are old, some are clever, some are simple, some are responsive, some are not. In speaking to so hetero-geneous a group of people as the average congregation comprises it is not possible for the preacher to define clearly what is known and what is unknown, what is the truth already accepted and what is the new truth to which he is pointing; for what is known and accepted by one may be unfamiliar and unacceptable to another, and what is unknown and new to one may be hackneyed and platitudinous to another. So the movement of a sermon cannot be simply a movement from the super-ficial to the profound, for the superficial will be merely boring to some and the profound (even if we achieve it) will be merely incomprehensible to others. Further, the pattern of the sermon constructed on this exclusive model will tend to show a movement from clarity and simplicity (which is good, however superficial) to obscurity and complexity (which is bad, however profound). Thus many of our hearers will become resigned to the fact that although we often start intelligibly they are going to lose the thread before the sermon is finished. Consequently the preacher's aim must be not merely to start simply and to end profoundly but rather to be communicating all the time at different levels of meaning.

There should be throughout the sermon a surface level of meaning immediately apparent even to the semi-comatose! Indeed even the semi-comatose should be able to grasp the theme of the sermon, the thing that can be stated in a simple sentence and that gives unity to the whole. I want to stress this: the sermon theme, the 'few notes' on which so much depends, must be simple enough for everyone to understand at least *at some level*. The simplicity of the theme should never be lost sight of as the sermon develops, and however profound the theological depths the preacher may try to plumb, to this simplicity, illumined by his exegesis of the Bible and of life the preacher should return at the end.

But while this simplicity is being enunciated and reiterated in different contexts throughout the sermon it should always be possible for the responsive and the sensitive in the congregation to find in that simplicity a relevance to the complexity of their own real life situation. Our simplicities should not be mere simplifications which are so often over-simplifications, falsifying and trivialising the deep things of the Gospel and of human life. On the contrary our simplicities (our themes) should contain an element of allusiveness, an open-endedness of imagery which allows what is being said to be cashed in the coinage of the infinite complexities of the individual human situation. So, while at one level, a simplicity is being reiterated, at another level a profundity is being discovered.

This may be a profundity of human experience or a profundity of theological insight or both. It need not, sometimes it should not, be *specifically* identified by the preacher. The profundities of private experience which the minister has shared with others in his pastoral work are not meant for public identification in the pulpit; but those who have shared that experience should know precisely what he is talking about. In the same way such profundities of theological insight as the preacher has discovered in his own reading should not always be publicly identified in the pulpit; but those who have read the same books should be able to recognise the theological problem he is grappling with even though that problem is never identified in the terms familiar to professional theologians. The need to identify the specific experiences one has shared or the specific books one has read can sometimes be a sign that the preacher has not really assimilated these experiences or these books into his own life-style and thinking. At the same time, unless these profundities of human experience and of theological insight are the soil out of which the sermon has grown, the preacher has nothing to say. Hence the need to keep that soil rich and fertile both by pastoral work and by reading. If this is done then, even while the preacher reiterates a simplicity, the responsive listener will sense that that simplicity is deep-rooted in an exegesis of life and of the Bible.

5. Some Hints and Helps
There are several further guidelines to which I want to refer very briefly before this section ends. The first concerns the use and abuse of illustrations. Some men have the marvellous gift of being able to find an apt story to illustrate almost everything they want to say. I especially envy that gift because I don't share it. I never seem to be able to remember the right story at the right

time. This is a real weakness, for a story-illustration from the preacher's own experience, or from biography, history or fiction—at best can make abstractions real and personal, generalities specific and relevant; and even at worst can provide a valuable variation in pace and tension within the sermon. Those of us who are weak in this department must be willing to learn from acknowledged masters of the art like Professor William Barclay who displays an almost profligate virtuosity in this regard. At the same time lesser mortals should beware! Even if you have a story to illustrate everything you say, not everything you say requires such illustration. There is no point in telling a story to illustrate what is already obvious. Again, a story, if it is not wholly relevant, is worse than useless. Yet again, a story told as true must *be* true and sound true, otherwise its effect will simply be to call in question the integrity of the preacher and hence the truth of his message. But when all this is said and important as these caveats are, the preacher must still recognise that illustration of *some kind* is essential. I want here to make a distinction which I believe to be of special importance to those of us who are not good at telling stories. Stories—personal, biographical, historical or fictional—are only one form of illustration and not necessarily the best. All that I have already described as exegesis of life is illustrative in its function, seeking to give substance and relevance to the Biblical truth toward which the sermon is pointing. Thus a superficiality of common experience can become an illustration of a theological profundity. Story illustrations are valuable but are not indispensable. What *is* indispensable (as I have already argued) is the kind of illustration contained in an exegesis of life without which the words of the Bible cannot become the Word of God.

Next, a word on a perennial problem—how far a sermon should be scripted. Here dogmatism is especially dangerous but some tentative guidelines may still be offered. Some preachers have a natural fluency with words. This is a great asset but a dangerous one. Speaking without script can become an excuse for speaking without thought. The man who finds it easy to keep talking must not suppose that because he is talking he is actually saying something! On the other hand the man who has no such natural fluency must not assume that in consequence he can never say anything important that he has not already written. Presumably he asked his wife to marry him without being fully scripted. Had he read her a prepared statement he might have said what he wanted to say more precisely but she would have been much less likely to accept him! Arguments like this, for and against scripting, can be multiplied indefinitely.

Let me try, however, to indicate (for what little it is worth) what my own practice has been. For the first nine years of my ministry, first as an Assistant in St. Giles' Cathedral in Edinburgh and then as a University Chaplain in Aberdeen, I wrote every word that I preached. Fortunately I only had to preach on average once every two or three weeks and in consequence I had time to write and re-write my sermons until I had on paper precisely what I wanted to say. I have not a fluent pen so it took me about fifteen hours for each sermon. Then I moved to my first charge, St. James' Forfar, which had 1700 members, no assistant and at least two services every week. Clearly time could no longer be found for a full script to be adequately prepared; and a full script ill prepared I found worse than useless since it made me say things that I could have said better without its help. In consequence, almost overnight I had to change course. The six or seven hours, which were all that I could now allow for the preparation of a sermon, had to be given up entirely to clarifying on paper the substance of *what* I was going to say. *How* I was going to say it I would not know precisely until the sermon was preached. I found to my immense relief that, if I really knew *what* I was going to say, *how* I was going to say it in large measure took care of itself. Confronted by a blank page in my study the right words were elusive and took many hours of hot pursuit to run them to earth. Confronted by a congregation within the context of worship surprisingly often the right words, so elusive in the study, seemed ready to volunteer themselves in the church. No doubt the words sought and found in the study would have been objectively more precise but I suspect that the words that volunteered themselves in church were more likely to communicate and find acceptance.

I would not dare draw any firm conclusions from evidence so flimsy and subjective as my own experience offers but I would like to make a tentative suggestion. I believe there are many men in the ministry of the church—many of the ablest—who have a latent capacity for extempore speech which has been inhibited by their own humility and intellectual integrity. Without loss of either precious virtue I believe that every man early in his ministry should seek to discover as honestly as he can in what measure he possesses this gift. He can start with an unscripted talk to the children, or an unscripted illustration in a sermon and having gained confidence there may move on to an unscripted Bible Study at a group meeting or an evening service. He may soon discover that his tongue is much less fluent than his pen. If so, he should simply thank God for his pen, use it to the full and forget about extempore speech. But he may find on the contrary that a fluency which is denied him at his desk is given to him in his pulpit. If so he should simply and very humbly thank God for that fluency and use it to the full.

Scripted or unscripted, however, the preacher must be very clearly aware of the difference between written and spoken English. (The kind of English I am using now is an awkward hybrid designed to do double duty—first to be spoken in a lecture room, later to be read in a book). The relative importance of words written to be *read* is conveyed by sentence structure. If the nuance of meaning is subtle, the sentence structure may require to be complex. Words written to be *spoken* convey their meaning, not primarily through sentence construction but through voice inflection, through variation of pitch, pace, tone-colour and volume. In ordinary conversation we use these variations of inflection naturally and in consequence we are able to make our meaning clear in spite of the fact that the grammatical structure of what we are saying is sometimes so primitive that we are not even making sentences. A verbatim transcript of almost any unscripted utterance, whether private conversation or public speech, soon makes clear that what is intelligible and persuasive when spoken can become confusing and dull when read. But the reverse is also true. The carefully wrought sentence with its subtle and complex balance of clauses, which so precisely conveys its meaning when *read*, can become confusing and dull when *spoken*. The *spoken* word is the preacher's instrument. If he is going to script in full he must constantly be asking himself not 'what does this look like on the page?' but 'what does this sound like when I say it?'

Since the sound of what is said is so important to

communication an intelligent use of the voice is essential. I do *not* mean that we are meant to become amateur actors. I *do* mean that we must try to reproduce in the pulpit the kind of voice inflection that comes to us naturally when we are out of the pulpit. This is not as easy as it sounds. If we are working from a script we must first be sure—as we have already seen—that the words we are using are the kind of words we would have used had we not been scripted. Further, in the pulpit we will usually have to speak slower, louder and more distinctly than we do in ordinary conversation. The preacher must consciously strive to retain his own natural voice inflection in spite of these limitations. Of course we must be audible, but not at any cost. The easiest way to be heard in a large resonant building, as the Church has known for many centuries, is to intone—to keep the voice firmly on one pitch and enunciate the words clearly at a level pace. By all means let the preacher enunciate his words clearly but not at one pitch or at a level pace. The preacher is under constant pressure, from the church building itself and from the hard of hearing who so often insist on sitting at the back of it, to intone his sermon. This pressure has got to be consciously and vigorously resisted. The natural inflection of the voice, which includes a wide variation in pitch, pace, tone-colour and volume, has got to be preserved at all costs—even, if necessary, at the cost of occasional inaudibility to the hard of hearing at the back of the church. In a large building a good modern sound-reinforcement system is essential if the preacher is to be allowed to sound like a human being and still be audible. But the only sure safeguard I know against the depressing influence of the pulpit on the human voice is for the preacher to be willing to face at least the occasional penance of listening to himself on a tape recorder. Often what he will hear will sound like a total stranger proclaiming the Good News with a broken heart.

I repeat: the aim of all this is not to turn the preacher into an actor but rather to enable him to retain his own personal integrity in the pulpit—to be himself—in spite of the pressures which constantly threaten to dehumanise him and so destroy the personal relationship between preacher and people within which the Word of God is heard. The importance of that personal relationship for the hearing of the Word was discussed at the end of the last chapter. Remembering what was then said, it should be apparent that the suggestions made at the end of this chapter concerning the choice of words and the use of the voice are not as trivial as might at first appear. They are the practical expression of an essentially theological concern.

4

WORKSHOP:
FOLLY EXEMPLIFIED

1. Recapitulation

This final section is the one I would have preferred not to have had to write. It will include a number of sermon outlines. It need hardly be said that these are not offered as models. They are simply specimens—some of them no doubt very bad specimens—of what I have found happens when I have tried to follow the theological and practical guidelines described in this book. This is an awkward and embarrassing task. A sermon outside the context of worship is a lame thing even when given in full. Sermon outlines scattered by the handful onto the printed page are not only lame but dead. Nevertheless I believe it to be dishonest to offer guidelines to others (however tentatively) and not to be willing to show where these guidelines have led oneself in practice. The purpose of this chapter is to do precisely that.

But first, in very brief summary, let me recapitulate what these guidelines have been.

1. Preaching must be Biblical and theological in content but must be expressed in terms of contemporary life, experience and language.

2. The preacher requires for his task all the intellectual resources he can muster. This is what his theological training is supposed to give him and both he and his teachers require constantly to be reminded that theology is for preaching.

3. Theology and ethics interpenetrate. In our proper desire to be kerygmatic and with our healthy fear of moralising we must not ignore the fact that preaching is addressed to the will and that many theological questions are being asked by our hearers in ethical terms.

4. The truth of the Christian Faith is something that is felt rather than thought by many deeply committed Christian people. Authentic feeling can be a means of grace no less than authentic thinking.

5. The preacher's task requires a double hermeneutic. He must be able to translate the language of Biblical theology into the language of contemporary life and experience. He must also be able to show that within contemporary life and experience God still speaks his Word—even though it is often heard in non-theological terms.

6. The hearing of the Word depends on the relationship of the preacher and congregation with God and with one another. Only within a personal caring relationship can we communicate in depth with one another and God with us.

In addition to these essentially theological considerations we have also examined certain practical guidelines for preaching.

1. For reasons theological and psychological as well as practical, strict unity of theme is essential.

2. Within this overriding unity a wide diversity of development is possible. Exegesis of the Text and 'exegesis of life' are two necessary elements in such development.

3. A sermon should move from the known to the unknown not only in thought but in language and imagery.

4. A sermon should be capable of acceptance in different modes—intellectual, volitional, emotional—and at different levels of insight from the superficial to the profound.

5. Every sermon requires to be well illustrated. But what I have described as 'exegesis of life and experience' *is* such illustration. Literary, historical or personal anecdotes may be useful but are not essential.

6. Since preaching is heard within a personal relationship of preacher and congregation the choice of words and how they are spoken must be determined by that relationship and so become the practical expression of an essentially theological concern.

Against that general background let me now condescend on specifics.

2. Beginning with the Text

What I want to do first is not to describe some ideal impossible for the hard-pressed preacher-pastor or even to concentrate on what we can sometimes do at our best. I am concerned with the average minister in the middle of an average week. I am assuming that neither the Christian Year nor his Lectionary has set him going, that nothing has happened in the life of the world, in his own personal experience or in his reading to trigger off an idea and that, confronted by an open Bible and a blank page, he has six or seven hours to prepare his sermon. What happens then?

Some years ago I used a tape recorder and a lot of scrap paper to keep a record of what actually *did* happen during the few hours that a not very distinguished sermon was under construction. Here (as honestly as I can) is a summary of what that recording and the accompanying notes showed. I need hardly repeat that this is no model. All I would claim it shows is that preaching is still possible even for the average minister in the average week—and that it can be an exciting and rewarding task, even at the very pedestrian level of achievement I am now going to describe.

It started (for lack of anything more immediate) from some previously noted verses, Mark 1:40–45, on which I realised I had not preached for many years.

'Once he was approached by a leper, who knelt before him begging his help. "If only you will," said the man, "you can cleanse me." In warm indignation Jesus stretched out his hand, touched him, and said, "Indeed I will; be clean again." The leprosy left him immediately, and he was clean. Then he dismissed him with this stern warning: "Be sure you say nothing to anybody. Go and show yourself to the priest and make the offering laid down by Moses for your cleansing; that will certify the cure." But the man went out and made the whole story public; he spread it far and wide, until Jesus could no longer show himself in any town, but stayed outside in the open country. Even so, people kept coming to him from all quarters.'

Preliminary reference to a reliable modern commentary makes it clear that in spite of some verbal ambiguity in the Greek text and a possible conflation, there are no obvious exegetical pitfalls to be avoided. This being so the mind is free to range over the passage until a theme emerges. It soon becomes apparent that the passage is crammed with homiletic material.

'If only you will you can cleanse me': compare this with Mk. 9:23, 'If it is possible for you, take pity upon us and help us'. One asks 'If you *will*' the other 'If you *can*'.

But Christ himself once said, 'If it is possible . . .' Mat. 26:39.

'In warm indignation Jesus stretched out his hand.' Was it anger or pity that moved Christ? 'Anger' seems the better attested reading. Then why was he angry? Where else do the Gospels record Christ's anger?

'Jesus touched him.' Against all the rules! There is an image here of the leper's contagion met by the contagion of Christ, perhaps an image of what the Incarnation means.

Yet no sooner is the cure effected than Jesus is saying 'Be sure you say nothing to anybody.' Why? 'The Messianic Secret' in Mark—the reasons for it and the significance of it.

'Show yourself to the priest and make the offering laid down by Moses'. Christ and the Law.

But the leper 'made the whole story public' oblivious to the need for reticence.

We now have a choice of themes any one of which may prove fruitful in development.
1. 'If you will; if you can; if it is possible.'
2. 'The anger of Christ.'
3. 'On Contagion': 'Jesus touched him.'
4. 'The Messianic Secret.'
5. 'A revolutionary's conservatism—Christ and the Law.'
6. 'Be sure you say nothing—the need for reticence.'

Undoubtedly the dramatic and emotional climax of the passage is found in the words 'Jesus touched him' and it was decided to explore first the image of Contagion. At this point in preparation the mind should be allowed to ramble and free association be given full play. What follows is the record of my own rambling.

Jesus touched him—that meant not only the risk of physical infection but that he was in some sense allowing himself to be defiled ceremonially and socially, even morally and spiritually. This was the cost of the leper's cleansing as the defilement of the Cross was the cost of ours. The law said keep your distance; but 'Jesus touched him.' It was outrageous. So was the Cross. But that outrageous compassion was the leper's cleansing and ours.

We must stop here for we are wandering from our central theme which is contagion; but note how in this story—and on the Cross—Christ both breaks the Law and fulfils it; and add this to the sermon theme already noted on 'Christ and the Law'.

We return to the theme of contagion, but this time as it relates to our world as well as to the world of the Bible.

We live in a contagious world. Disease, poverty, war all 'touch' us as never before. We try to meet the threat by 'keeping our distance', by isolationism—economic, political, religious, national, social, personal. All of us are involved in segregation and apartheid in one form or another, building our 'middle walls of partition' (Eph. 2:14 AV), our 'dividing walls of hostility' (NEB).

We must stop again, for if we pursue this further we shall lose our central image (contagion) and hence the essential unity of the sermon.

'*We live in a polluted world,* polluted by us; and we threaten in our space-probes to pollute other planets. Is it possible that our world has been polluted from the outside as the elaborate quarantine precautions for the first returning lunar astronauts suggested—the 'Quatermass' science-fiction theme become science fact? Is Man solely responsible for the evil he finds on this planet or have we been contaminated from beyond it? Is it after all *literally* true what Paul says: 'Our fight is not against human foes but against cosmic powers, against the authorities and potentates of this dark world, against the superhuman forces of evil in the heavens'? (Eph. 6:12 NEB). Is that just mythology, theological science-fiction, or is it a plain statement of a Biblical doctrine we have demythologised out of existence? We can't be sure. But whether or not Satan has touched this planet Christ has.

What do we believe about Christ in the Universe in the space age?

O be prepared my soul!
To read the inconceivable, to scan
The myriad forms of God those stars unroll
When, in our turn, we show to them a Man.

Christ in the Universe: Alice Meynell

Let us stop there (for again we are wandering from the key image) and let us return from outer space to 'inner space', from the cosmic to the personal.

Suffering is contagious. How we throw words across the six-foot gap that the Law of Prudence requires.

Sometimes the touch of a hand can do more, or one of the many trivial sacraments of love which we turn to when words fail us. 'Thy touch has still its ancient power' (see Hymn 52 in the Church Hymnary, Third Edition). And when the woman with the haemorrhage touched Jesus in the crowd he knew that 'power had gone out of him' (Mk. 5:30). 'Who touched me?' asks Jesus and the woman knew she was no longer anonymous.

But again we must stop or we shall lose our unity of theme.

Sin is contagious. Once again we throw across the six-foot gap our condemnation, our advice, our sympathy even. But we don't want to get too close in case we might catch something. Anyway, we *have* all caught something—through our solidarity in sin. We are Adam and 'As in Adam all men die, so in Christ all will be brought to life' (1 Cor. 15:22).

We must stop again or we shall lose the central image; but notice that the Adam-Christ text suggests that there are good contagions as well as bad.

The contagion of faith. 'Christianity is caught not taught.' The need for personal contact within the Church and between the Church and the world. How we isolate ourselves in case we catch something. (Individual Communion cups may be a symbol of this—but be careful or some people will hear nothing in the whole sermon but this one outrageous suggestion!)
'The Church is meant to be the fellowship within which you catch the Spirit as you might catch the

'flu—"let us thine in-flu-ence prove". (Influence and influenza are derived from the same root.) We fight that influence like the plaose but still it spreads within the Church and beyond it. . . .'

At this point our exercise in free association can end Clearly we already have abundant material even though we have firmly suppressed any development, however promising, which might threaten the unity of the structure. But we must now arrange the remaining material in the most effective order, which is seldom the order in which it is originally conceived. This sermo was first preached when rival American and Russian inter-planetary space probes were about to be launched and when the threat of contamination *of* the earth or *by* the earth was being widely discussed in the media. This was accoy chosen as the first counterpoint to the text, and, at a theological level, as a finishing point as well, thus emphasising the unity of the whole sermon. The final structure, with the key sentences italicised, emerged as follows,

Text in context (Mark 1:40-41)
The law said 'Keep your distance or run the risk—physical, social, spiritual'. But Jesus touched him. The scourge of leprosy in the ancient world. How the Levitical law dealt with it. (O.T. Lesson, Lev. 13—see especialty verses 1-8 and 45-46). Rough-and-ready diagnosis regarded many skin diseases as leprosy which were occasioned by other causes—some no doubt psychosomatic. But that is not the point. The cutting edge of the incident was that Jesus was confronted by a man no-one else would touch with a barge pole. But Jesus touched him, meeting the ugly contagion of the leper's body with the healing contagion of his own compassion.

We live in a highly contagious world. World Health Organisation stretched to the limit. And other sinister contagions of our own invention now threaten. Nuclear testing. World trade recession. Other people's diseases, wars, poverty, all 'touch' us as never before. We try to isolate ourselves, nation from nation, to keep our distance, but it never works.

Make it personal. Other people's suffering is contagious. That's why most of us try not to get within six feet of it (according to the law of prudence). But only when we get close enough to those we would comfort to feel the contagion of their suffering are we close enough for them to feel the contagion of our compassion.

Other people's sin is contagious. That's why we prefer not to get within six feet of it. We seldom allow ourselves to get really close to the unlovely spiritually sick folk we all know—close enough to 'touch' them.

But if sin and suffering are contagious—so are other things—courage, enthusiasm and laughter. *Other people's faith is contagious.* 'Christianity is caught not taught.' It is a kind of good infection. We are supposed to catch it in church. This is what 'the fellowship of the Holy Spirit' is all about—'Let us thine in-flu-ence prove!' 'Influence' and 'influenza' are both derived from the same root!

But we are so afraid of catching anything that we isolate ourselves one from another even in our worship and then wonder why it's so sterile. Sometimes, indeed, *the Church has itself been an agent of inoculation against the Christian faith*—enabling people to be only very superficially infected by it, not enough to cause any real inconvenience, just enough to ensure that they never catch the real thing. *Yet for twenty centuries the Divine infection has been spreading.* Men have resisted

94

it like the plague, inoculated themselves against it, but still it spreads.

We live in a highly contagious world. Do we perhaps also live in a highly contagious universe? *Is it perhaps possible that this world of ours is subject to contagions, good and evil, which come from beyond itself?* It's scientists now, not theologians, who are talking about that—about the dangers of contaminating other planets, or of being contaminated by other planets. We know that one touch of man uncleansed on a virgin world could so contaminate its natural form of life as to twist and pervert it for ever.

Then what of *our* world? *Do we perhaps live in a world contaminated from outside?* Or is that just so much theological science fiction? *We can't be sure. But whether or not Satan has touched this planet, God has.* Of that we *can* be sure. Through that Divine contagion something irreversible happened. When Christ was born God touched the leprous face of human history. If you or I were God we wouldn't touch this world with a barge pole. But God embraced it, with arms outstretched on a Cross.

The sermon has now been stripped down so that its essential unity of theme is apparent. The italicised words show that it is about contagion and nothing else. Developments of the theme which would confuse that central image have all been suppressed—including some of our most promising material. But what is suppressed is not to be discarded. We have already noted six possible sermon themes stemming directly from Mark 1:40–45. We must now notice that a further seven possible themes have emerged as we have worked over the one selected from the original six. These are:

(a)   Segregation, reconsiliation and the dividing wall of hostility;

(b)   Cosmic sin and cosmic redemption—Christ and the new cosmology;

(c)   Human sacraments of love and Holy Communion;

(d)   'Virtue had gone out of him'—the cost of compassion;

(e)   'Who touched me'—an end to anonymity;

(f)   'As in Adam . . . so in Christ'—corporate guilt and corporate salvation;

(g)   'The Koinonia of the Holy Spirit'.

All of these themes stemmed directly from our development of the contagion image yet they can be seen to contain a very great diversity of homiletic material. Had this material been incorporated into the sermon 'On contagion' the result would have been both confusing and wasteful; confusing because it would have imperilled the unity of the theme, wasteful because much of the material we have pruned away will prove to be cuttings which carefully transplanted can establish a life of their own. I don't mean to suggest that every sermon we prepare magically creates another thirteen to follow it. Some of the thirteen inhibited themes will continue to be inhibited because we have already preached them in other and better contexts. Others will refuse to take root on their own when we try to transplant them. But some will flourish and may well become healthier specimens than the plant from which they were originally pruned. The discovery that this really happens is a great strength and encouragement to the hard pressed pastor-preacher—especially at the beginning of his ministry. In spite of his fears to the contrary he finds he has plenty to say. He must simply learn not to try to say it all at once.

3. Beginning with Life

Barth speaks of the preacher's Scylla and Charybdis: of the necessity of finding one's way between 'the problem of human life on the one hand, the content of the Bible on the other'. We have already seen what happens when we start with the text of the Bible and reach out from that to the problems of life. But it is no less legitimate to start with a problem of life and then to ask what the Bible has to say about it. Of course there are obvious dangers in this procedure. The preacher may simply take a human problem, give his own answer to it, search for some Biblical justification for the answer he was going to give anyway and, having found it, call the whole a sermon. But there is no need for this parody of preaching to result. A sermon that starts from a problem of human life can be as Biblical a sermon as one that starts from the text of the Bible and may indeed be a better sermon since it starts where people are. But this will only be so if the real life problem is brought honestly to the Bible with the desire to discover what is the characteristically theological and kerygmatic thing the Bible has to say about it. One can, of course, hope to find much that is best and most profound in contemporary humanist insight anticipated and confirmed in the Bible. But one must not attribute to the Bible contemporary answers which it does not give. More, one must expect that, in some measure at least, the Bible will contradict the findings of contemporary humanism and, even where it agrees with these findings, will transcend them. But once again we must be honest. Artificial tensions between humanist and Christian answers to the problems of life must not be invented just for the sake of argument. Where humanist and Christian agree, as they often do, we must thank God for it, so long as both agree with the Word of God.

Let us see how this works out in practice. Let us suppose that the preacher has decided to prepare a sermon on 'Frustration'—a very real problem of contemporary human life concerning which contemporary humanist thought has a lot of helpful things to say. How will the sermon develop? The first draft may run something like this:

'There is a growing sense of futility in contemporary human life, personal and national. In some measure we all feel frustrated—illustration here is all too easily come by. What causes these frustrations? How do we cope with them? Are they inevitable, perhaps even potentially constructive; or are they always inhibiting and life-denying? Here is our Scylla, a problem of human life crudely sketched. Now for Charybdis. What does the Bible have to say about frustration? Ecclesiastes is an obvious starting point. "I have seen all the deeds that are done here under the sun. They are all emptiness and chasing the wind" (Eccl. 1:14). A re-reading of the passage from which these words come soon shows that Ecclesiastes has stated the contemporary problem of frustration with classic precision and power. But if he has any answer to the problem it is certainly not a Christian answer. What then does the New Testament have to say? Romans 8 is a natural place to turn for help and a verse from the NEB translation soon leaps out of the page. "The created universe was made the *victim of frustration* not by its own choice but because of him who made it so" (Rom. 8:20). So God is at work in our frustrations. Are the psychologists perhaps pointing to the same thing when they talk of sublimation? Is Christ himself the supreme victim of frustration, the Cross the symbol of a frustration that God made sublime?'

A problem of human life and the content of the Bible

98

have now been allowed to interpenetrate and the outline structure of a sermon has begun to emerge. We must now tidy up and strengthen the structure and begin to put flesh on the bones. The sermon is going to be built on the tension between the verse in Ecclesiastes and the verse in Romans. Both texts should first be given and the sermon outline proceed something like this:

' "All is emptiness and chasing the wind." Typical Ecclesiastes. A marvellous man with a marvellous mind, honest and rational; but profoundly cynical and pessimistic. "Life is a vain futile business. You try to be good, clever, rich, happy—it gets you nowhere, for you just go round in circles (says Ecclesiastes). In the end nothing matters: whether you're good or bad, clever or foolish, happy or sad, rich or poor, death will have you at the last and all your striving will mean nothing." All very frustrating—as you'd expect for Ecclesiastes. At first sight Paul seems to agree: "The created universe was made the victim of frustration." But the Romans passage explodes into an exuberant hope. There is a purpose in the frustration because it is God who is frustrating us.'

The texts have now been set briefly in their contexts and in juxtaposition. Their relevance to the contemporary problem of frustration must now be made explicit. So the outline will continue:

'Whoever is responsible for the frustrating, God or the Devil, is doing a great job. We're all victims of frustration. You try (like Ecclesiastes) to be clever or rich or happy and its all "chasing the wind". Some of us even try to be good only to find (like Paul) that that too is "chasing the wind". Everywhere its the same. There's the frustration of the married woman who gave up a good job matched by the frustration of the career woman who never got married. It seems you can't win! And what's true of us as individual people is no less true nationally and internationally. (Illustrations of economic political frustration at home and abroad are legion and in preaching are specified). "I have seen all the deeds that are done here under the sun. They are all emptiness and chasing the wind." Yes Indeed. *But*: "The created universe was made the victim of frustration not by its own choice but because of him who made it so." That means that in some sense it is God who is frustrating us—frustrating our sin and our selfishness and the primitive desires within us that threaten our destruction; frustrating us in our barbarous power politics and our crazy economics. Why? Because there is some great new thing that God is leading us toward and he will not let us rest content until we attain it. "Victims of frustration" we may be but "I reckon that the sufferings we now endure bear no comparison with the splendour, as yet unrevealed, which is in store for us" ' (Rom. 8:18).

The problems of human life and the two texts from the Bible have now become tightly interwoven and the Romans text has suggested the key image that will focus the theological content of the sermon—Christ the victim of frustration, the Cross both the symbol of that frustration and of Christ's victory over it. The way through to this final theological thrust comes from an unexpected quarter, from the language of contemporary psychology. The sermon outline proceeds thus:

"Frustration" in contemporary psychological

jargon often goes with another word "sublimation", the redirection of our lower instincts into new and creative channels. "Sublimated" means literally, "made sublime". So frustration can be the stuff out of which the sublime can be made. (When will the apostles of the permissive society learn the facts of life?) Of course life is frustrating but, as Paul says, "It is God who made it so." For his purpose is to take this fallen human nature of ours and, having frustrated our sin, to remould us into new people more like Christ, to rechannel our energies and desires, to take the crude stuff that is our nature and by grace to make of it something sublime.'

The sermon is now poised between the problem of human life and the content of the Bible ready for the final theological thrust. The conclusion will be as follows:

'The story of Christ's life and ministry is a story of increasing frustration, the Cross the climax of that frustration and its supreme symbol. The Cross is the symbol of the frustration of God by human sin, Christ the victim of that frustration. Some who saw the frustration of God on Calvary must have gone home echoing Ecclesiastes words: "I have seen all the deeds that are done here under the sun. They are all emptiness and chasing the wind". But those who saw it thus missed the point. For God sublimated his frustration, made it sublime. "The head that once was crowned with thorns is crowned with glory now" '.

(Once again I must repeat that this is not offered as a model of how to construct a sermon: it is simply offered as a typical specimen of what happens in one man's

101

mind when an attempt is made to follow the theological and practical guidelines which this book has been talking about and which were summarised at the beginning of this final section).

4. Some Further Examples in Brief

I have taken two sermon themes, one on 'Jesus touched him' the other on 'Victims of Frustration' and have examined their construction at some length. In the first case starting from the text of the Bible I concentrated on showing how the central theme had to be isolated from associated themes clustered round it before it could become relevant and effective in the real life situation. In the second case, starting from a problem of life, I have tried to show how a theme once chosen may be developed in such a way that an exegesis of life becomes an exegesis of the Bible. Let me now try to indicate very briefly how each of these specimen outlines can be paralleled in a variety of different contexts. Following the pattern of the 'Jesus touched him' theme I shall suggest some similar passages from both Old and New Testaments where the Biblical narrative appears to acquire an extra dimension once its relevance to the problems of human life is recognised. Then, following the pattern of the 'Victims of Frustration' theme I shall suggest some contemporary life situations the theological significance of which lies just below the surface ready to be illuminated by the text of the Bible and in turn to illuminate that text. These will be purely random samples, no more than a suggestion of the kind of ground that is worth prospecting by the preacher who is looking for the Word of God both in the problems of human life and in the text of the Bible.

(a) 'The Image Makers' (Exodus 20:4)

Take first a typical Old Testament theme: the condemnation of idolatory. Focus it on the Second Commandment or on the story of Aaron and the golden calf, or on any one of scores of passages in the Old Testament where the image-makers are pilloried.

'Who were the image makers? They were the popular theologians of the ancient world, skilled craftsmen who talked theology in language people could understand and who were prepared to put their undoubted talents at the disposal of whatever religion the establishment said was the right one. Their job was to present an acceptable image of God to men.

The image maker is still very much in business only now its an acceptable image of *Man* to men that he offers to create. The contemporary image maker is the P.R.O. man, the creator of the public images.

But just as the old image makers failed to create a true image of God to men so the new image makers are failing to create a true image of *Man* to men.

So we're left to our do-it-yourself image making; theologians and humanist alike.

Or, at least, we would be if Christ had not taken over the work of the image makers, old and new. He offers a true image of God to men and a true image of Man to men. . . .'

(b) 'Hope Deferred' (Revelation 22:20)

Take now a recurrent theme of the New Testament: the expectation of the early return of Christ to earth. Revelation 22 offers an obvious and eloquent statement of the theme.

'Three times in the last chapter of the Bible the promise is given: "Yes, I am coming soon" (Rev. 22:6,

12, 20) and the Bible ends with the passionate cry "Come Lord Jesus". Only he didn't come. You'd have thought in consequence the Christian Church would have folded up in despair and disillusionment. But it didn't, for as the early hope receded a greater hope grew.

The hope of these early Christians in the imminent return of Christ was an illusory hope. Sometimes God uses our illusory hopes, lets them grow and wither, because sometimes only so can a larger hope come to flower.

That was the pattern with the apostles during Christ's earthly ministry. They had their illusory hopes. And so have we.

Sometimes illusory hopes are the prelude not to disillusionment but to discovery. Columbus sailed west in the firmly held belief that he was fulfilling instructions given by the Prophet Isaiah and when he got to Cuba he thought he had reached Japan. Thus the New World was discovered sailing west on an illusion! God uses our illusions to lead us to new worlds we never dreamed existed.

Some of us couldn't go on without our illusions, some of us would never have got started. Columbus would never have left port if he'd known he was heading the wrong way for the Indies.

But we can't live for ever on our illusions. As the illusory hopes of the early Church receded so a greater hope grew—a hope for this world, and for the world to come.'

(c) 'Christ both died and rose' (Romans 14:9)
Take now the insistence of the New Testament on both the death and the resurrection of Christ against those on the one hand who said he hadn't really risen and those on the other hand who said he hadn't really died. We

104

may take as text Romans 14:9. 'Christ both died and rose'.

'The disciples were convinced the Cross was the end. Then something happened big enough to change their lives and through them to change the course of history. When people asked them what had happened they always gave the same answer: "Christ is risen." I believe that—as a matter of fact.

But: it's the faith that's not quite sure of itself that's always looking for miracles, for something external to itself to compel belief. "Give us a sign," they said. "Come down from the Cross." But he wouldn't do it.

After his death Christ did not give the kind of sign he had refused to give during his life. What you believed depended on how you interpreted the facts—the fact of the Cross and the fact of the Empty Tomb—and how you interpreted the facts depended on your attitude to the man who had died.

Some people (the Caiaphas party) accepted the Cross but tried to explain away the Empty Tomb. Some people (the Docetic party) accepted the Empty Tomb but tried to explain away the Cross. Paul and the apostles stood firm. "Christ both died and rose."

In every age the same drama of attitudes is played out. You cannot explain away the dark mystery of that Cross, his, or yours, or your loved one's. But neither can you explain away the bright mystery of resurrection, of good out of evil, of life out of death; not the little resurrection miracles of our own experience, of losing our life to find it, of dying to live. The Cross and the Empty Tomb belong together. "He both died and rose."

That's how it was for the apostles. That's how it must be for us.'

105

(d) 'Massah, the Place of Proving' (Exodus 17:7)

The next sermon theme starts not from the text of the Bible but from a problem of human life.

'How can we "prove" God? How can we know that he's there and that he cares?

There's a kind of scientific proof, which we know we'll never get and we can understand why we'll never get it.

But there's another kind of proof we feel we ought to have: the assurance that when we're up against it God won't let us down, that he will prove himself not as the conclusion to our arguments but as the answer to our needs.

That's exactly how the Israelites felt at Massah. Massah means "the place of proving". They were up against it in the wilderness and they reckoned it was time for God to prove himself. "Is God in our midst or not?" they asked (Exodus 17:7).

That incident became for later Old Testament and New Testament writers the classic example of how *not* to prove God: "You must not challenge the Lord your God as you challenged him at Massah" (Deut. 6:16); or the same words echoed by Christ himself "You are not to put the Lord your God to the test" (Mat. 4:7).

Why not? Because the attempt to prove that someone loves you ends inevitably in tragedy or farce. All Othello ever proved about Desdemona was his own faithlessness toward her. That's all we'll ever prove about God using Othello's methods.

Yet we *can* prove God, not as the conclusion to an argument or the result of an enquiry but as the consequence of a commitment. Commitment comes first and is the basis of every "proved" friendship. You don't make an equation of your friend's kindness or an experiment of your wife's faithfulness. So it is with God.

But in one vital respect the human analogy fails. We can only prove God once we recognise that he is proving us, questioning, trying, judging us through the duties and demands, the strains and stresses that are the staff of life. We have lost our sense of the reality of God because we've been so busy trying to prove him we haven't noticed how he is proving us.

"Is God in our midst or not?" Sometimes you doubt it when, like the Israelites, you find yourself without water in the middle of a desert. Sometimes all of us have been at Massah, the place of proving. But, even as in our foolishness at Massah we try to prove God and fail, can we doubt that he is proving us or that in the end he who proves us will strengthen us, he who judges us will save us, he who has led us through the desert will give us the water of life we crave for.'

(e) 'Therefore and Nevertheless" (Hosea 11:8)
Finally, here is an example of a sermon theme starting neither from the text of the Bible nor from a problem of life but from a remembered phrase in theological reading. Karl Barth says that the heart of the Gospel is 'not a natural "therefore" but a miraculous "nevertheless" '.

'Take two passages, Hosea 11:1-9 and Romans 3:26. Each leads you to expect a "therefore" and then offers instead a "nevertheless'. Hosea makes his ruthless indictment of Israel: *nevertheless* "How can I give you up Ephraim, how surrender you, Israel?" (Hosea 11:8). Paul makes his even more ruthless indictment of all mankind; *nevertheless* "all are justified by God's free grace alone" (Romans 3:24).

107

We specialise in "therefores"—"therefores" in the natural world, in the moral world, and (hopefully) in the religious world as well. The search for "therefores" has been the making of the scientific technological civilisation we enjoy today. All of that is good, for God specialises in "therefores" too. Our logic is only the palest reflection of his.

But that's not the Gospel. At the heart of the Gospel, as Barth says, lies "not a natural therefore but a miraculous nevertheless". So the miraculous "nevertheless" of Hosea and Paul becomes God's word to us: we are justified by the faith that is love; not just our love for God, but his love for us. For love's "nevertheless" can create value even in worthless things. Don't let's spoil it by letting the Law with its "therefores" creep back in.

The miraculous "nevertheless" is the coinage of love, divine and human. God loves us not because we're worth it but because his love gives us worth. So with our love for one another; romantic love can live for a little on "therefores"; real love can live only on "nevertheless"—as in the song from the old musical *Show Boat:*

> "Maybe he's lazy, maybe he's slow
> Maybe I'm crazy, maybe I know,
> *But* (nevertheless!) I can't help lovin' that
> man of mine."

"Can't help loving that Man of mine" is one of God's favourite songs! "How can I give you up, Ephraim, how surrender you, Israel?" '

5. In Conclusion

These arid sermon summaries must bring this discussion to a close. I would have preferred to end less lamely with some suitably high-minded and carefully worded theological generalisation. But that would have been dishonest. 'Theology is for Preaching' has been the theme of this book and it is appropriate that it should end humbly with the very raw material of preaching itself. Of course it is true that a sermon summary read clinically out of context is a poor substitute for a real sermon preached person to person in the context of worship. That may partly explain why these summaries read so badly. Another less happy explanation may simply be that they are summaries of bad sermons. But there is one final and good reason why the stuff of preaching examined clinically often looks a little disappointing. To quote once more the Authorised Version's inspired mistranslation, part of 'the folly of the Gospel' is the 'foolishness of preaching' and 'it pleased God by the foolishness of preaching to save those who believe' (1 Cor. 1:21). That mistranslation must never be used as an excuse for our incompetence but it does make some kind of sense and sanity out of the folly to which we are a party Sunday by Sunday in our pulpits, and it is as good an answer as any to those who call in question the value of the whole enterprise. As I said at the beginning (and as must now be abundantly clear), I don't understand preaching. But I believe in it as I believe in the Church of which it is a function.